GEORGIA

Michael Spilling

MARSHALL CAVENDISH

New York • London • Sydney

Reference edition published 1998 by
Marshall Cavendish Corporation
99 White Plains Road
Tarrytown
New York 10591

Originated and designed by
Times Books International, an imprint of
Times Editions Pte Ltd

Printed in Singapore

Library of Congress Cataloging-in-Publication Data:
Spilling, Michael.
    Georgia / Michael Spilling.
       p. cm.—(Cultures of the World)
    Includes bibliographical references and index.
    Summary: Describes the geography, history, government,
economy, people, lifestyle, religion, language, arts, leisure,
festivals, and food of a Caucasian republic with a turbulent
past.
    ISBN 0-7614-0691-3
    1. Georgia (Republic)—Juvenile literature. [1. Georgia
(Republic)] I. Title. II. Series.
DK672.3.S68   1998
947.58—dc21   97–16570
                          CIP
                            AC

INTRODUCTION

SEPARATED FROM RUSSIA by the magnificent Caucasus mountains and washed by the warm waters of the Black Sea, the Republic of Georgia is a newly independent country not to be confused with the American state of the same name.

Georgia is an ancient land with a long and complex history, fascinating culture, and rich artistic heritage. Called *Sakartvelo* ("sa-KART-ve-lo") in the country's native tongue, the Republic of Georgia was until 1991 a part of the Soviet Union. This fiercely independent Caucasian republic is known for its wine, sunny climate, spectacular mountain scenery and—more infamously—as the birthplace of the dictator Stalin.

Georgia is geographically at the crossroads where Europe meets Asia and where Christendom meets Islam; the Greeks, Byzantines, Persians, Arabs, and Russians have all left their mark. Consequently, it is a land of many peoples and languages, but despite these diverse influences, the proud and hospitable Georgians have retained a tenacious sense of their own traditions, religion, language, and identity.

CONTENTS

Government building in the capital, Tbilisi.

CONTENTS

In mountainous regions, the lifestyle is simpler and more traditional than in the lowland and urban areas.

GEOGRAPHY

FORMERLY A PART OF THE SOVIET UNION, this small, recently independent republic is situated in the heart of the Caucasus mountain range, on the eastern coast of the Black Sea. It is separated from its giant northern neighbor, the Russian Federation, by the main range of the Caucasus, while bordering Azerbaijan to the east, Turkey to the south, and Armenia to the southeast. Surrounded by mountains and sea, the country is geographically self-contained and this has helped it to preserve its national identity and culture despite numerous foreign invasions.

Although it is largely mountainous (87% of the total area), Georgia has a remarkably varied climate ranging from the subtropical Black Sea coast to the ice-capped peaks of the Caucasus. This variety is even more noteworthy considering Georgia's relatively small size, covering an area of 26,900 square miles (69,670 square km)—slightly smaller than South Carolina or about the same size as the Republic of Ireland.

Left: **Batumi waterfront facing the Black Sea.**

Opposite: **A mountainous road winds through tranquil surroundings in the Caucasus.**

Mt. Kazbek, an extinct volcano, is the second highest peak in the Caucasus.

FROM MOUNTAIN PEAKS TO SWAMPY LOWLAND

Georgia can be roughly divided into three main geographic areas: the Great Caucasus range, central lowlands, and Lesser Caucasus.

THE GREAT CAUCASUS Higher than the Swiss Alps, the Great Caucasus dominate northern Georgia. The mountain belts rise from the east and are often separated by deep gorges.

The Bokovoy range is northernmost; farther south the most important spurs are those of the Lomisi and Kartli ranges. The cone of Mt. Kazbek, an extinct volcano, dominates the Bokovoy range at a height of 16,512 feet (5,030 m). Georgia's spectacular crest-lined peaks also include Mt. Shkhara (16,627 ft/5,066 m), Mt. Tetnuld (15,918 ft/4,850 m), and Mt. Ushba (15,420 ft/4,698 m)—all in the region of Upper Svaneti—and

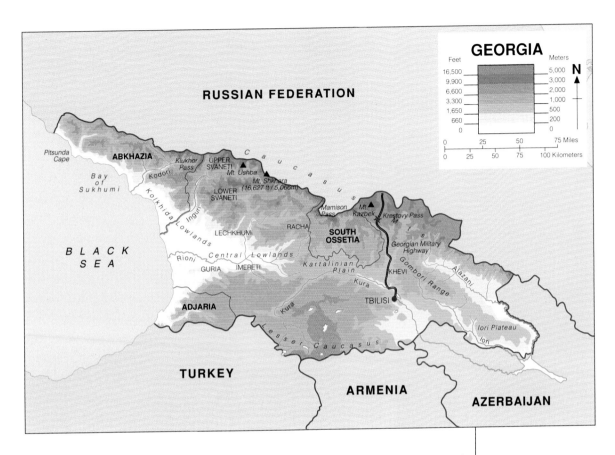

Mt. Rustaveli (16,273 ft/4,958 m) to the southeast. The wooded gorges and valleys in bloom have been a great lure to poets and travelers through the ages, including the Russian writers Alexander Pushkin, Mikhail Lermontov, Lev Nikolaevich Tolstoy, and Maxim Gorky, as well as the French writer Alexandre Dumas.

Lermontov, for example, in describing the Krestovy Pass in his novel, *A Hero of Our Time* (1840), wrote: "What a delightful place, that valley! On all sides rise inaccessible mountains, reddish cliffs hung over with great ivy crowned with clumps of plane trees; tawny precipices streaked with washes, and far above the golden fringe of the snows …"

Few roads traverse the Great Caucasus; the scenic Georgian Military Highway that links Georgia to Russia is the best known. Other routes over the mountain range include the Mamison Pass in Racha and the Klukhor Pass in Abkhazia.

CENTRAL LOWLANDS   The southern slopes of the Caucasus merge gradually into Georgia's central lowland areas. The Kolkhida lowlands are to the west, spreading from the shores of the Black Sea. Many of Georgia's major rivers rush down from the slopes of the Great Caucasus across the Kolkhida lowlands to the Black Sea. These include the Kodori, Inguri, and Rioni. The Rioni River is thought to be the Phasis of Greek legend, along which Jason and the Argonauts traveled to capture the Golden Fleece. At one time, the lowlands were mostly swampland. A development program that constructed drainage canals and river embankments improved the region so that it is now an important area for growing subtropical crops such as tea and citrus fruits. The climate is hot and damp.

THE GEORGIAN MILITARY HIGHWAY

The 128-mile (206-km) Georgian Military Highway cuts north through the Great Caucasus range to connect Georgia with Russia and beyond. Beginning in Tbilisi, this road crosses the precipitous mountains to reach Vladikavkaz in southern Russia.

The route was known since ancient times and provided an important trade link between Europe and Asia. For many centuries it was dangerous, and in winter often impassable. It rises to an impressive height of 7,983 feet (2,432 m) at the Krestovy Pass, actually the lowest and easiest route over the Caucasus. The route offers the traveler fantastic views of the surrounding mountains and river valleys.

Today's road was originally built by the Russians to improve communications with their new subject territory. It was completed in 1817 by the Russian regional commander, General Alexie Yermelov (1772–1861), on the orders of Tsar Alexander I. The name of the route originates from this time, when the Russians used the road to move troops to aid their conquest of Transcaucasia.

The Likhi mountain range forms a bridge between the Great and Lesser Caucasus, and marks the division between the east and west of the country. To the west of the Likhi range, the Kartalinian Plain forms an arid plateau, situated between Khashuri and the ancient capital of Mtskheta. This central plateau extends along the Kura River and its tributaries. The Kura River is the longest in Transcaucasia, beginning in northeast Turkey, passing through central Georgia, and running the whole length of Azerbaijan before flowing into the Caspian Sea.

The easternmost part of Georgia is formed around the Alazani River valley and the Iori Plateau, both of which are divided by the Gombori mountain range. The Alazani valley is Georgia's chief grape-growing and winemaking region.

THE LESSER CAUCASUS Southern Georgia is marked by the ranges and plateaus of the Lesser Caucasus that divide Georgia from its southern neighbors, Turkey and Armenia. The highest peak of the Lesser Caucasus is Mt. Didi-Abuli (10,830 ft/3,300 m).

The densely populated urban areas of Tbilisi (*above*) **and Mtskheta are located in the Lesser Caucasus, close to neighboring Turkey, Armenia, and Azerbaijan.**

Opposite: **The Georgian Military Highway runs from Tbilisi to the northern border.**

REGIONS

Georgia is an ethnically diverse country and regional identity is important to the various peoples. Traditionally it has been divided into a number of geopolitical regions: Abkhazia, Upper Svaneti, Lower Svaneti, Lechkhumi, Racha, Samegrelo, Guria, Adjaria, Imereti, Meskheti, Tori, Dzhavakheti, Trialeti, Inner Kartli, Lower Kartli, Zrtso-tianeti, Khevi, Mtiuleti, Pyavi, Khevsureti, Tusheti, and Kakheti.

Historically, Imereti and Samegrelo formed the nucleus of western Georgia, while Kartli and Kakheti formed the rump of eastern Georgia. Regions such as Upper and Lower Svaneti, Khevi, and Khevsureti are mountainous and lightly populated.

Today the only recognized and separate regions within Georgia are the autonomous republics of Abkhazia and Adjaria on the Black Sea coast, and the autonomous region of South Ossetia.

Opposite: **The capital city of Tbilisi is an industrial area with an active private sector.**

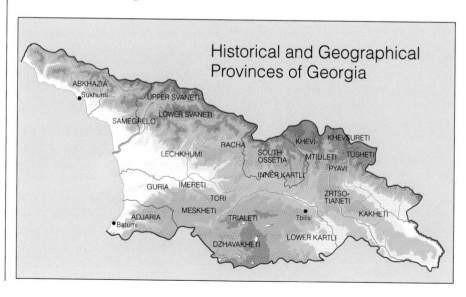

Historical and Geographical Provinces of Georgia

SVANETI

Upper and Lower Svaneti have the most inaccessible and difficult terrains in Georgia. Upper Svaneti is wholly mountainous, with a small population of about 15,000. Lower Svaneti has a population of 12,000. Mestia, the chief town of Upper Svaneti, was not accessible to cars until 1935 when the road was widened with dynamite.

Situated 7,220 feet (2,200 m) above sea level in the region of Upper Svaneti, Ushguli is the highest continuously inhabited village in Europe. Like many other centers in Svaneti, the village is striking because of the more than 20 medieval watchtowers that dot the landscape. The surrounding mountain scenery is superb, with good views of the nearby peaks of Ushba and Shkhara.

CITIES

TBILISI With a population of 1.3 million, Tbilisi, the capital of Georgia, is the country's most populous city. It is a long, narrow city that straddles both banks of the Kura River. The city is built on several hills and is protected on three sides by mountains.

Founded in A.D. 458 by King Vakhtang Gorgasali, Tbilisi was named after some nearby hot sulphur springs and means "warm." The city, situated at a crossroads between Asia and Europe, reflects the influences of both continents. Ruled by both Muslims and Christians at different times in its checkered history, Tbilisi has a cosmopolitan, multiethnic character that is reflected in its architecture, which ranges from the Moorish-style Opera House to medieval churches and Baroque Russian architecture.

The city's main, tree-lined thoroughfare—Rustaveli Avenue—is named after the 13th century Georgian poet, Shota Rustaveli. Georgians have always venerated their poets more than other artists.

Tbilisi is also an industrial city and accounts for more than 35% of the country's industrial output. It has had a subway system since 1966.

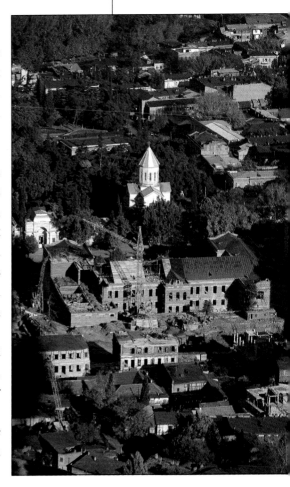

Gelati Monastery in Kutaisi was built in the 12th century by King David the Builder to celebrate his early victories against the Seljuk Turks.

KUTAISI Kutaisi is situated near the Rioni River in the central lowlands and is the capital of the Imereti region. It has a population of 240,000, making it the second largest city after Tbilisi. Legend has it that the capital city of King Aeëtes, custodian of the Golden Fleece, was situated here. The Rioni River—known in ancient times as the Phasis—is navigable all the way to the Black Sea and would have allowed Jason and his Argonauts access to it. Kutaisi is known to have existed as a Greek colony in the 7th century B.C., and was the capital of Georgia from 978 to 1122. It contains impressive medieval structures such as the Cathedral of King Bagrat, Gelati Monastery, and the Monastery of Montsameta—all built during the "golden age" of King David the Builder and Queen Tamar.

OTHER CITIES Batumi (population 140,000), the capital of the autonomous region of Adjaria, is Georgia's most important port on the southern Black Sea coast. It began as a port under the Romans and reached its height of prominence in the Middle Ages, but was devastated by the Turks in the 16th century. Modern Batumi is a city of parks with subtropical vegetation, a broad stony beach, and high-rise tourist hotels. Despite the town's wet climate, it is a popular holiday resort, especially with Russian tourists. Sukhumi (population 122,000), the capital of the autonomous region of Abkhazia, is situated on the Bay of Sukhumi. Like Batumi, it is a popular resort town; unlike its southern counterpart, it has a sunny climate. Other major towns include Rustavi (Georgia's main industrial center), Poti, Khashuri, Tskhinvali (the chief town of South Ossetia), and Gori.

CLIMATE

Georgia has a varied climate, ranging from subtropical humidity to snow and ice. The Great Caucasus form a barrier that protects Georgia from cold air from the north, while the west of the country is open to warm, moist air from the Black Sea. Western Georgia has a damp subtropical climate with heavy rainfall all year. The rain is heaviest around Batumi in the south. Winters in the west are mild and warm, and the temperature never falls below 32°F (0°C). Along the Black Sea coast, the temperature rarely falls below 40°F (4°C). Eastern Georgia is cut off from the warm air of the Black Sea by the Likhi mountain range and consequently has a drier, more continental climate.

Altitude has an important climatic influence. Most of the Caucasus are above 6,000 feet (1,800 m) and have an Alpine climate, lacking a true summer. Many of eastern Georgia's mountains are more than 11,000 feet (3,300 m) above sea level and covered with snow most of the year.

15

FLORA AND FAUNA

Georgia's varied landscape has created an unusual diversity of flora. The country has approximately 5,000 types of wild vegetation, and 8,000 types of fungi, ferns, and moss. More than a third of Georgia is covered by forests and brush, and the vegetation varies from east to west.

Some flora in western Georgia is subtropical. Alder trees predominate in the swampy coastal areas of the Kolkhida lowlands. Farther inland, where the climate is drier, the forests include oak, chestnut, beech, and liana. The Pitsunda pine can be found in Abkhazia. A grove of these unique trees is protected in a national park on the Pitsunda Cape.

Eastern Georgia has fewer forests and is dominated by grasslands dotted with prickly undergrowth. The lowlands and foothills are forested only along the rivers, especially the Kura, Iori, and Alazani, where oak, poplar, and willow trees can be found. In the higher, wetter regions juniper, pomegranate, Georgian maple, and pistachio trees grow well.

Georgia's unique geographical location has resulted in a mixture of European and Asian fauna with 100 mammal, 330 bird, 48 reptile, 11 amphibian, and 160 fish species. There are gazelles, deer, and wild boars in eastern Georgia's lowlands. The dwarf shrew, an endangered species, can be found only around Tbilisi.

The western lowlands of the country have a greater diversity of fauna. A variety of mammals can be found here, such as moles, squirrels, brown bears, badgers, weasels, deer, wolves, foxes, lynx, mink, and wildcats. Birds of this region include pheasants, geese, curlews, ducks, cormorants, and woodpeckers and, during migration, pelicans, storks, herons, hawks, and eagle owls.

The alpine areas of Georgia are inhabited by many species of birds including the Caucasian jackdaw, black grouse, pheasant, cuckoo, woodpecker, and magpie. Goats and Caucasian antelope can also be found in the mountains, and the rivers are full of trout. The Black Sea has a rich diversity of sea life including dolphins, sharks, salmon, herring, dogfish, and swordfish.

"Nature here is astounding to the point of despair. If I lived in Abkhazia for as much as a month, I think I'd write half a hundred exquisite tales."

—From a letter by the Russian playwright, Anton Chekhov

Opposite: **The fallow deer. Georgia is rich in wildlife.**

PHEASANTS (PHASIANUS COLCHICUS)

Pheasants are indigenous throughout the Caucasus and southeast Europe. They are larger than quail or partridge and most are long-tailed birds of the open woodlands and fields, although some prefer grain fields near brushy cover. All have hoarse calls and a variety of other notes. The males of most species are strikingly colored, while the females are more inconspicuous. Courting males sometimes fight to the death in the presence of hens.

Many pheasants are kept in private collections and are also raised for sport in some game reserves. Some species have been brought to the verge of extinction by hunting. Legend has it that pheasants were first introduced to Greece and from there to the rest of Europe by Jason and the Argonauts when they returned home from their arduous adventures. It is thought that the name "pheasant" derives from the River Phasis, now called the Rioni River, down which the Argonauts traveled when they escaped from Colchis with the Golden Fleece.

HISTORY

MANY PEOPLE THINK of Georgia as a small part of the former Soviet empire, not realizing it has a rich and ancient history of its own. Georgia is situated at a geographical crossroads between Europe and Asia, and as such shares the complicated and turbulent history of the Middle East.

This fiercely independent Caucasian republic has often been dominated by greater neighboring powers—Byzantium, Turkey, Persia, and most recently, Russia—which have all left their mark. Despite these influences, Georgia has retained an uninterrupted and powerful national identity, culture, and language.

EARLY HISTORY

Remains of an anthropoid ape discovered in Georgia suggest that the Caucasus were one of the birthplaces of human life. Archeological excavations and the discovery of cave drawings along the Black Sea coast suggest human existence around the middle Paleolithic period (150,000–40,000 B.C.). Paleolithic man lived in caves or earth dugouts and survived mainly by hunting animals and gathering fruits and berries. A Neolithic culture existed in Georgia from 5,000 to 4,000 B.C. The Neolithic inhabitants were hunters, fishers, and food gatherers.

Bronze Age man thrived in Georgia between the third and second millennium B.C. It was about this time that Georgian metallurgy developed and Georgian metalworkers became the most renowned in the ancient world.

Above: **Turkish storyteller in the days when the Turks ruled vast areas of Transcaucasia.**

Opposite: **Highway palace of Queen Tamar, who extended ancient Georgia's borders during her rule in the 12th–13th centuries.**

19

An ancient carving (c. 5th–8th centuries B.C.) on stone from the Iberian period.

At the end of the third millennium B.C., the Kurgan people invaded the Caucasus from the Eurasian grasslands. Elements of this Kurgan culture fused with those of the local people to form the famous Trialeti culture in the region southwest of Tbilisi. Remarkable finds in Trialeti show it was inhabited by cattle-raising tribes whose chieftains were men of power and wealth. Burial mounds have been discovered dating from 2,100–1,500 B.C., many of them containing vessels of gold and silver.

COLCHIS AND GREECE

The historical records of the Assyrians provide the first concrete evidence of the rulers and tribes of Georgia. The western part of Georgia, then known as Colchis, was famous in ancient history and mythology. It was first mentioned in Assyrian records in the 12th century B.C. From the 8th century B.C., the place was visited by the ancient Greeks, who had set up colonies and trading stations all around the Black Sea.

THE IBERIANS

Around 730 B.C., the Cimmerians and Scythians from the north attacked Georgia and occupied Colchis and much of the Caucasus. Their invasions scattered many of the ancestral tribes of Georgia into the remoter mountain regions and pushed some of them into the Persian sphere of influence. However, the Tibareni and Mushki tribes managed to reestablish themselves in eastern Georgia by the time Alexander the Great crushed the Persians at the battle of Arbela in 331 B.C. The two tribes then merged with local tribes to form the kingdom of Iberia, with its capital at Mtskheta. Here, for the first time, a common Georgian language was developed, and Mtskheta, situated 20 miles (32 km) north of modern-day Tbilisi, thrived at the crossroads of a busy trade route that linked Greece to the west with India and China to the east.

In 66 B.C. the Romans, under the command of Pompey, conquered Iberia and the resulting Roman influence brought many advantages to the Iberians. These included new roads and increased trade with the rest of the Roman empire. Soon Iberia established such good relations with the Romans that it was considered an ally rather than a subject state.

CONVERSION TO CHRISTIANITY

The Iberians embraced Christianity in A.D. 330 during the reign of the Roman emperor Constantine the Great. The conversion is attributed to Saint Nino, a woman who was said to possess healing powers. Political conditions favored the adoption of the new religion—it was the official creed of the still-powerful Romans, and neighboring Armenia had converted 30 years earlier. In the 5th century A.D., King Vakhtang Gorgasali (reigned 446–510) strengthened the Iberian church by establishing an independent bishop at Mtskheta, which remains the center of the Georgian Orthodox Church today. The king also moved his capital to Tbilisi in 458, thus founding the capital city.

To the west of Iberia, Lazica, a kingdom that had sprung up from the ruins of Colchis, adopted Christianity in the 6th century. For much of the 6th and 7th centuries, Lazica and Iberia found themselves at the center of a power struggle between Byzantium to the west and Persia to the east. The struggle ended when the Arabs, inspired by the new Islamic faith, swept through Persia and the region, capturing Tbilisi in 645.

The Byzantine and Persian empires fought over Georgia between the 6th and 7th centuries. Genghis Khan invaded in 1220, and Turkey and Persia sparred over Georgia in the 16th century. Four centuries later Soviet armies invaded the country in 1921, and Georgia remained a part of the Soviet Union until it declared its independence on April 9, 1991.

THE ARGONAUTS' QUEST FOR THE GOLDEN FLEECE

The earliest version of the legend was told by Apollonius Rhodius in his epic poem, *Argonautica*, composed in the third century B.C. Greek geographer Strabo (63 B.C.–23 A.D.) also tells of the golden fleece in his literary work, *Geography*. Many details in the *Argonautica* have since been supported by archeological evidence, suggesting that the Argonauts' journey may have been more than just a legend.

According to the story, Jason, a Greek prince, set out with a band of 50 men in their ship, the *Argo*, to find the fabled golden fleece. The throne belonging to his father had been usurped by his uncle, Pelias, and Jason could only regain his rightful crown by proving his bravery. In the search for the golden fleece, the Argonauts encountered many dangers along a long and eventful journey that finally took them to Colchis.

There, Aeëtes, the Colchian king, refused to give up the fleece unless Jason went through several trials. First, he had to tame the king's fire-snorting bulls and yoke them to a plough, which he achieved through strength and cunning. Following this, he had to plough a field and plant a helmetful of dragon's teeth, each of which sprang up into armed warriors, whom he had to defeat. Here, Aeëtes' daughter Medea, a sorceress who had fallen in love with Jason, stepped in to help. She advised him to throw a stone among the warriors, causing confusion so that they turned in anger upon each other and fought to the death, leaving Jason victorious.

Aeëtes, however, still refused to part with the fleece, which was being guarded by an ever-watchful dragon. Once again, Medea went to Jason's aid by guiding him to the fleece and casting a spell on the dragon, causing it to sleep. This allowed Jason to escape in the *Argo* with both the fleece and Medea.

ARAB DOMINATION

The Arabs were not interested in colonizing Georgia, and Georgian culture and the Christian religion were allowed to flourish. Georgian princes were allowed to rule, but under Arab supervision. Tbilisi soon became the center of several important international trade routes dealing in goods from Russia, Daghestan, and the Middle East.

In the 9th century, the Bagratid clan came into prominence. The Bagratids were to unite Georgia under a single crown and hold power for the next 1,000 years, ending only with Russian annexation in 1801. The first Bagratid ruler, King Ashot I (reigned 813–830), was appointed ruler of much of southern Georgia. Under King Bagrat III (975–1014) the eastern and western parts of Georgia became unified for the first time: it is only from this time that Georgia can be referred to as the single entity we know of today. Under King Bagrat IV (1027–72) Georgia became one of the most powerful states in the Caucasus.

Constantinople was the capital of the powerful Byzantine empire, which fought against the Arabs for control of the Georgian region then known as Iberia.

King Giorgi II could not cope with Turkish threats and handed over the running of the kingdom to his son.

DAVID THE BUILDER

In the 11th century, the Seljuk Turks pushed westward, capturing Persia and Armenia, and invading Byzantium. The Byzantine army was crushed at Manzikert in 1071. The son of King Bagrat IV, King Giorgi II, reigned from 1072 until 1089, when, unable to deal with the onslaught of the Turks, he abdicated the throne. His 16-year-old son, David (1073–1125), took over.

Under King David, known as "The Builder," national unity was restored and trade, culture, and religion flourished. King David resisted the Turks, winning many brilliant victories between 1110 and 1122, and defeating them decisively at the battle of Didgori in 1121. Tbilisi was recaptured from the Turks in 1122. The king's humane treatment of the Turkish Muslim population set a standard of tolerance in his multiethnic kingdom.

King David also managed to extend Georgia's territory as far as the Caspian Sea and captured parts of Armenia as well. His campaigns were indirectly aided by the timely arrival of the European Crusaders in Palestine. The Crusaders captured the Holy Land in 1099 and were a constant threat to the Islamic world throughout the next few centuries, allowing Georgia to develop its own culture and reinforce and extend its borders without Arab interference.

QUEEN TAMAR

The great works of King David were continued by his great-granddaughter, Queen Tamar (reigned 1184–1212). Christian culture flourished and many religious buildings were constructed, among them the Vardzia Caves. With the fall of the Byzantine empire in 1204, Queen Tamar was able to extend the boundaries of Georgia westward along the Black Sea coast and create the independent empire of Trebizond. Under Queen Tamar, the Georgian feudal system reached its high point and the virtues of chivalry and honor were celebrated in Shota Rustaveli's (1172–1216) epic romance, *The Knight in the Panther's Skin.*

THE MONGOL YOKE

The Mongol invasion of Transcaucasia in 1220 brought Georgia's "golden age" to an end. Led by Genghis Khan, the Mongols swept across much of Asia and eventually threatened the borders of Europe. The Mongols were an aggressive, well-armed, and well-trained army of horsemen notorious for their cruelty and bravery. Queen Tamar's heir, King Giorgi IV Lasha (reigned 1212–23), was killed in battle against the Mongols. The Mongols dominated Georgia for the next century, taxing the Georgians heavily.

King Giorgi V (reigned 1314–46), called "The Brilliant," took advantage of weakening Mongol power to regain Georgian independence. Unfortunately the Mongol lord, Tamerlane (1336–1405), in the course of his campaigns against the Turks and Persians, created much havoc and destruction from which the kingdom never fully recovered. Georgia was overrun on eight consecutive occasions; towns and churches were ruined and the people fled to the hills.

Portrait of Queen Tamar found in the Vardzia cave complex in the Lesser Caucasus.

A 19th century engraving of Abbas I, Shah of Persia.

OTTOMAN TURKEY AND SAFAVID PERSIA

In 1453, the Ottoman Turks captured Constantinople, isolating Georgia from European Christendom. At the end of the 15th century, the rise of the Safavid Persians posed a further threat to Georgia, which found itself caught once more between two expanding empires to the east and west. Both Turks and Persians encroached upon Georgian territory until, in the Peace of Amasia in 1555, Georgia was divided into spheres of influence—the Turks controlled western Georgia while the Persians controlled the eastern part. The Georgians were powerless to resist.

In 1578, the Turks overran the whole of Transcaucasia, but were subsequently driven out by the Persian Shah Abbas I (reigned 1557–1628). The Georgian people were heavily persecuted for their Christian beliefs and many were deported to distant regions of Persia (Iran), where their descendants can still be found today. Queen Ketevan of Kakheti was given the choice of abandoning the Christian faith and entering the shah's harem, or suffering a cruel martyrdom. She chose to die for her faith and is numbered among the saints of the Georgian church. For the next 200 years the kings of Kartli, as eastern Georgia was then known, ruled only through the will of the Persian shahs.

RUSSIAN ANNEXATION

In the early 18th century, the Bagratid kings, Taimuraz II (reigned 1744–62) and Herekle II (1720–98), were able to rebuild Georgia in its own image, and not that of Persia's. Persian power was waning and the Russians were expanding into Transcaucasia. Nevertheless, Persian-backed Muslim raiders from north of the Caucasus and Daghestan had a crippling effect on Georgian trade and industry. It is estimated that the population of Georgia may have been reduced by as much as half by the end of the 18th century because of these attacks. King Herekle II, convinced that his isolated Christian kingdom could not hold out against an assortment of Muslim enemies, then sought the aid of Christian Russia.

In 1783 Russia and Georgia signed the Treaty of Georgievsk. Under the agreement Georgia became a Russian protectorate, renouncing all dependence on Persia. Despite Russian promises of protection, Tbilisi was again sacked in 1795 by the Persians and 50,000 of its inhabitants killed. Herekle II, the 75-year-old king, fought in the battle and narrowly escaped capture. He died in 1798.

In 1800 Herekle II's son, the invalid King Giorgi XII, decided to hand over the kingdom to the care of the Russians unconditionally in exchange for their full protection. That same year the king died. He was the last ruler of the 1,000-year-old Bagratid dynasty. In 1801 the Russian tsar, Alexander I, confirmed that Kartli and Kakheti were a part of the Russian empire and abolished the Bagratid monarchy.

Memorial to the Treaty of Georgievsk signed between Russia and Georgia on August 4, 1783.

Tsar Alexander I's expansionist program brought the regions of western Georgia under Russian rule.

GEORGIA UNDER THE TSARS

Under Tsar Alexander I, the Russians continued their expansion into the Caucasus, waging war against the Turks, Persians, and Lezgian tribesmen of Daghestan. Russian power brought stability to Georgia, and under the guidance of the gifted and enlightened Russian viceroy, Michael Vorontsov (1782–1856), industry and trade prospered, and communications improved. In 1872 a railway was built to link Tbilisi with Poti, and factories, mines, and plantations were developed by Russian and Western entrepreneurs.

With increased communication, however, came change; the Russian social administration replaced the old Georgian feudal system, and Russian education and culture became widespread. Many Georgian intellectuals reacted against Russian influence. The "Men of the '60s" were a group of radicals and social activists, full of the new social democratic ideals then current in Europe. Although tsarist Russia did not permit any organized political activity, social issues were debated in journals and local assemblies, and through works of fiction.

The 1890s saw the appearance of a new group of radicals who had absorbed the political ideals of Karl Marx while studying abroad. They were called the *tergdaleulni* ("terg-dal-e-UL-ni"), meaning "those who had drunk from the river Terek," an act that symbolized their going out into the world, beyond the boundaries of Georgia. The leader of this group was Noe Zhordania (1868–1953). Another prominent member was Joseph Dzhugashvili, better known as Joseph Stalin.

WAR AND REVOLUTION The failed 1905 revolution in Russia led to social unrest and industrial strikes in Georgia that were brutally suppressed by Cossacks, a group in southern Russia that fought for the tsarist army. In 1914 Russia entered World War I, fighting against the Germans and Austrians. The Russian army collapsed in 1917 amid economic disintegration, severe food shortages, and social upheaval at home. This was followed by one of the 20th century's most momentous events, the Russian Revolution in November 1917. Under the leadership of Vladimir Lenin (1870–1924), the Bolsheviks seized power.

In Georgia the power vacuum was filled by the Social Democratic Party led by Noe Zhordania. The country regained its autonomy for the first time in 117 years and maintained a neutral stance throughout the Russian Civil War of 1917–20, but its independence was short-lived. In February 1921, following victories throughout Russia, the Bolshevik 11th Red Army marched into Georgia, driving Zhordania and his government into exile. Georgia was once more in the grip of its more powerful neighbor.

Soldiers of the 1917 revolution, when the Bolsheviks seized power from the tsarist authorities.

JOSEPH STALIN (1879–1953)

Perhaps the most famous and notorious Georgian of modern times, Stalin was born in Gori, Inner Kartli. Originally christened Joseph Vissarionovich Dzhugashvili, he adopted the name Stalin, meaning "man of steel," when he turned to revolutionary politics. Stalin's family was poor and his father a drunkard. Despite great hardship, his mother succeeded in sending him to an Orthodox seminary in Tbilisi, where he trained for the priesthood. He was expelled in 1899; it is suspected that this was because he was propagating Marxism.

Although anti-tsarist, Stalin was never a nationalist. He did not believe Georgia's salvation lay in independence but in becoming a part of a larger political structure. He became active in Georgia's revolutionary underground and was arrested and imprisoned many times and exiled to Siberia twice by the tsarist authorities. He became friends with Lenin and was at the forefront of the 1917 Bolshevik Revolution. When Lenin died in 1924, Stalin's power was such that he was able to isolate and disgrace his political rivals. In 1928 he exiled his main political rival, Leon Trotsky (1879–1940), and gained absolute control of the Communist Party.

Stalin was a cruel, ruthless, and dictatorial ruler responsible for the imprisonment or death of many millions of Russians through the forced collectivization and political purges of the 1930s. It is estimated that as many as 20 million Soviet citizens died as a result of his policies. Nevertheless, he gained a reputation as a great war leader, leading the Soviet Union to victory over the Germans in World War II. He died in 1953 in mysterious circumstances, probably from a brain hemorrhage.

SOVIET GEORGIA

Georgia was at first incorporated into the Transcaucasian Soviet Federated Republic in 1922, along with Armenia and Azerbaijan. The Georgian Social Democrats, still popular despite their earlier defeat, organized a rebellion in 1924 that the communists put down. Seven thousand people were executed and Soviet rule was finally established in Georgia.

In 1936 Georgia became one of the 15 republics of the Soviet Union. Joseph Stalin, a native Georgian, ruled the Soviet Union from 1928 to 1953.

Despite the fact that he and his chief of police, Lavrenti Beria (1899–1953), were Georgians, Stalin treated his homeland harshly.

During World War II (1939–45), the Georgians helped defend the Soviet Union against the German invasion of the northern Caucasus. German paratroopers were dropped into Georgia to aid the German advance, but were promptly caught by the local militia. The German advance was thus stemmed.

Soviet economic policy forced the collectivization of all agricultural workers, as had happened throughout the Soviet Union. Georgia was converted from a largely agricultural economy into an industrial and urban society. Following Stalin's death in 1953, a private, freewheeling "second economy" developed, providing goods and services not available in the planned state economy. Far from the center of power in Moscow, the Georgians were able to grow their own crops privately and run their own cottage industries.

In 1945, after the defeat of Nazi Germany, it was a Georgian soldier, with a Russian comrade, who hoisted the Soviet red flag over the seat of German power, the Reichstag.

31

Ousted president Zviad Gamsakhurdia's supporters lobbying for him.

RECENT HISTORY

In the late 1980s, the Soviet Union underwent fundamental political and social changes under the leadership of Mikhail Gorbachev (b. 1931). In the new atmosphere of *glasnost* (openness), political and social freedoms were reinstated.

In April 1989 demonstrations in Tbilisi to demand independence were brutally suppressed by Soviet special troops and 20 civilians were killed. After the event, however, the massacre was reported by the Soviet authorities to have been a mistake. Soviet president Gorbachev had not ordered the suppression; the decision had been taken by the local government and army commanders. It was partly due to this event that the Soviets began to lose control of the country: anti-Soviet sentiment was fueled by the suppression and speeded up the move toward independence. There was little the Soviet authorities could do other than launch a full military invasion, which would have been highly impractical and unpopular in the unstable social and political climate of the time.

Soon, new political parties appeared. Free elections held in 1990 were won by a coalition called the Round Table led by a former dissident, Zviad Gamsakhurdia (1939–94). Georgia was declared independent on April 9, 1991, and Gamsakhurdia elected president of the new republic. However, his authoritarian rule made him unpopular. Civil war broke out in late 1991 and a military council deposed him in 1992. The military council soon handed power to a State Council of various political parties headed by Eduard Shevardnadze (b. 1928). Shevardnadze had served as Soviet

foreign minister under Gorbachev. Despite terrorist attempts to kill him in August 1995, elections held in November that same year confirmed him as president for a further five years.

The Soviet Union disintegrated in 1991 and the Commonwealth of Independent States (CIS) was formed, consisting of the 15 newly independent countries of the former Soviet Union. Georgia joined the CIS in 1993.

Life for independent Georgia has not been peaceful or trouble-free, and it still has much to do to establish stability in one of the most volatile regions in the world. In South Ossetia rebels have been fighting a war for independence against Georgian forces; they seek unification with North Ossetia in Russia. In Abkhazia sporadic fighting has continued since 1992. Near Georgia's borders, conflicts continue in Nagorno-Karabakh between Georgia's neighbors Azerbaijan and Armenia, and an uneasy peace has held since the end of 1996 in neighboring Chechnya.

Fighting in Chechnya has contributed to the climate of instability in the Caucasus.

GOVERNMENT

GEORGIA HAS HAD LITTLE political stability since gaining its independence in April 1991. For the first time in 70 years, it was free and self-governing, and many Georgians wanted a strong, centralized state to reinforce this newfound independence. Unfortunately, ethnic unrest and separatist revolts have resulted in a turbulent political situation that is only just beginning to stabilize under the leadership of Eduard Shevardnadze.

The Georgian republic includes two autonomous republics and one autonomous region: the Abkhazian Autonomous Republic, the Adjarian Autonomous Republic, and the South Ossetian Autonomous Region. These regions were originally formed by the Soviet administration as semi-independent homelands for ethnic minorities. They have limited self-government but have proved to be hotbeds of ethnic tension and conflict for the fledgling Georgian republic. It is estimated that over 20,000 people have died in regional and ethnic conflicts in Georgia since 1991.

RECENT EVENTS

For 70 years Georgia was a part of the Soviet Union and had no independent government. A Georgian parliament did exist—the Georgian Supreme Soviet—but as the national branch of the Communist Party it could only implement decisions made centrally by the Communist Party leaders in Moscow.

Above: **Abkhazian refugees awaiting evacuation by United Nations helicopter.**

Opposite: **Guards on patrol in Mtskheta.**

35

Eduard Shevardnadze's early political exposure comes from his term as Soviet foreign minister in the 1980s.

Amid the disintegration of the Soviet Union, free elections were held in 1990 and Zviad Gamsakhurdia swept to victory. However, his dictatorial methods led to his swift exit from power in early 1992. Eduard Shevardnadze, the chairman of the State Council, was temporarily elected and an emergency constitution passed. Gamsakhurdia continued his opposition to the new government before dying in mysterious circumstances in early 1994. Shevardnadze was democratically confirmed as Georgia's leader in presidential elections held on November 5, 1995. He gained 70% of the vote, making him president for a further five years. A shrewd politician with vast international experience, he has sought to modernize Georgia and forge closer economic ties with the West and the other newly independent republics in the Caucasus and Central Asia. Having served as foreign minister in Mikhail Gorbachev's Soviet administration in the 1980s, his international stature has ensured that Georgia's problems are gaining attention from other world leaders.

THE 1995 CONSTITUTION Prior to the elections in 1995, a new constitution was drawn up based on many of the main principles of the country's 1921 constitution. The new constitution confirmed Georgia as a democratic state where all citizens are equal. The constitution protects basic human rights such as freedom of speech and thought, freedom of religious practice, and the freedom to own property. The 1995 constitution has replaced the hastily created interim constitution of November 1992.

PARLIAMENT

The Georgian parliament is a unicameral body consisting of 235 members elected by proportional representation—150 from single-member constituencies and the rest directly from party lists. Each member is

Government House in Tbilisi.

elected for a four-year period. Parliament and other main government ministries are situated in the Government House of the Republic of Georgia in the center of Tbilisi. Citizens must be at least 18 years old to vote in national elections, and 25 years old to run as deputies.

The president, as head of state, is elected for a term of five years and cannot serve more than two terms. He chooses his Council of Ministers (cabinet) and, along with the ministers, holds supreme executive power.

THE GEORGIAN FLAG

Georgia's national flag was first used when the country declared independence in 1917 amid the upheaval of the Russian Revolution. The flag was resurrected in the late 1980s with the breakup of the Soviet Union, and in 1991 it became the official flag of the newly independent Georgia. The deep maroon red is the national color of Georgia. The black stripe represents the country's tragic past while the white stripe symbolizes hopes for a bright future.

Georgians celebrating
state independence on
May 26.

POLITICAL PARTIES

The Communist Party of Georgia was disbanded in 1991 following the
collapse of the Soviet Union. Dozens of political parties were then formed,
based mainly on regional or nationalist loyalties, or kinship ties, and often
with military backing from paramilitary or neogovernment groups.

The situation remained uncertain until parliamentary elections were
held, along with the presidential election, in November 1995. In Georgia's
current parliament, no one political party has an overall majority.
Shevardnadze's Citizens' Union of Georgia (CUG) is the largest party,
having won 23.7% of the votes and gained 91 parliamentary seats. The
National Democratic Party and the All Georgian Union of Revival are the
next two largest parties, having gained 7.9% and 6.8% of the votes
respectively. Eight other parties are represented in parliament, although
none holds a significant number of seats. The breakaway region of
Abkhazia is led by the Abkhazian Popular Party (APP).

CONFLICTS IN ABKHAZIA AND SOUTH OSSETIA

The Abkhazians have been actively campaigning for independence for their region, the Abkhazian Autonomous Republic, since 1989. The Abkhazians have been in the region for 2,000 years and are ethnically different from Georgians; they are Muslims and have their own language. Through successive waves of migration during the 19th and 20th centuries, they have become a minority in their own country and now make up only 18% of the population.

In August 1990 Abkhazia's parliament, without its Georgian members, voted to separate from Georgia. However, the Georgian government ignored the declaration. In 1992 Abkhazian troops seized much of northern Abkhazia. A ceasefire was eventually established with the help of the United Nations and Russian mediation. In September 1993 Abkhazian separatist troops violated the ceasefire by sweeping southward and capturing Sukhumi. Georgian government forces were driven out of the region and the separatists declared Abkhazia liberated from Georgia. As a result, 270,000 ethnic Georgians fled Abkhazia to western Georgia.

Above: **President Boris Yeltsin (center) of Russia and Georgian president Eduard Shevardnadze (right) at a press conference following the Georgia-Abkhazia summit held in Moscow in September 1992.**

Top: **Refugees from the armed conflict in South Ossetia.**

An American charity supplies food and household goods to an Abkhazian refugee.

A number of United Nations-led negotiations have since been held, but to date there has been no settlement. The conflict has so far been contained within the borders of Georgia but has the potential to spill over and destabilize the region. Abkhazia is deemed an autonomous area, but this is to some extent merely a title, and separatists continue to campaign for an independent status for the region.

In the South Ossetian Autonomous Region, Ossetians have also been campaigning for separation. In 1989 the people demonstrated in support of Abkhazian separatist demands. The Ossetians speak their own language and, like the Abkhazians, are Muslims. They want greater control over their own affairs and eventually to unite with North Ossetia, a part of the Russian Federation. The South Ossetian legislature declared itself an independent republic in 1990, in an attempt to have equal status with Georgia within the former Soviet Union. However, the Georgian parliament refused to recognize the Ossetian declaration of independence.

In 1991 the Ossetian parliament passed a resolution in favor of integration into the Russian Federation. Tensions led to violent clashes between Ossetians and ethnic Georgians in the region, and Georgian government troops were involved. Several thousand people were killed and many South Ossetians fled across the border to North Ossetia to escape the violence. In 1992 a ceasefire was declared and this has been observed up to the present time. The ceasefire was established with Russian participation.

UNDER ARMS

Before 1991 Georgia's security was provided by the Soviet army, in which many Georgians served as conscripts. Following independence two distinct military groups emerged in Georgia. The National Guard was formed to support the government, while a group called the *Mkhedrioni* ("m-ked-RIO-ni"), led by Dzahba Iosseliani, was formed to fight against the secessionist Abkhazians. However, the *Mkhedrioni*, numbering 7,000 men, soon developed into an independent force answerable only to their leader.

As a newcomer to the political scene, Shevardnadze was unable to control these groups when he first came to power in 1992. In 1995 the *Mkhedrioni* was implicated in an attempt to assassinate Shevardnadze. Since then, it has lost much of its power and has, to some extent, been kept in check by the increasing stability of Shevardnadze's government. Today, it still carries out illegal activities but no longer operates as a government-sanctioned military force.

A regular Georgian army has developed only gradually and faces many difficulties. There is a professional army of 20,000 partly made up of former members of the National Guard and defectors from the *Mkhedrioni*. A further 500,000 Georgian men have previous military experience gained as conscripts in the Soviet army before Georgian independence. The armed forces have up to 120 tanks and 50 combat aircraft.

The Ossetian conflict is difficult to resolve. The Ossetians want unification with North Ossetia, while Georgians refuse to accept the loss of what they consider to be a part of their traditional homeland.

ADJARIA—HAVEN OF STABILITY

Adjaria has been Georgia's least troubled self-governing region since independence, and has not seen the extensive and bloody conflicts experienced in Abkhazia and South Ossetia. Despite their ethnic Georgian origin, the Adjarians retain a strong sense of separate identity, mainly because of their adherence to Islam. Most Georgians in the region converted to Islam during the long period of Ottoman rule.

Adjaria did not become a part of the Russian empire until as late as 1878, and was granted autonomy by Soviet Russia as part of an agreement with Muslim Turkey in 1921. Following the breakup of the Soviet Union, many Christian Georgians regarded Muslim Adjaria's autonomy as a threat to a unified Georgian nation. Tensions increased in 1991 when Georgia's first president, Zviad Gamsakhurdia, announced his intention to end Adjaria's autonomous status. Mass demonstrations took place in Batumi, and when elections were held in 1991, parties in favor of Adjarian autonomy swept the board.

Since 1991 Aslan Abishidze has led Adjaria's local government and runs the region virtually as a personal fiefdom. Tbilisi has effectively lost administrative control of Adjaria, although the Adjarian leadership has made it clear that it desires to remain a part of Georgia. Eduard Shevardnadze has since attempted to appease the Adjarians and has complimented them as a model of stability in a turbulent part of the world.

Economically, Adjaria has proven to be one of Georgia's most successful regions. The Adjarians have not been affected by the conflicts

that have disrupted so much of Georgian life, and cross-border trading is flourishing with fellow Muslims in Turkey.

Soviet troops and an armored vehicle patrolling the streets prior to the breakup of the Soviet Union in 1991.

RELATIONS WITH RUSSIA

Despite early conflicts of interest, Russia and Georgia have developed constructive relations based on shared goals. Both countries would like to see their mutual border secure and the secessionist conflicts in Abkhazia, Ossetia, and Chechnya brought to a lasting settlement.

Following the breakup of the Soviet Union, Russia has been keen to maintain an influence in the Caucasus region. Georgia has made various concessions to Russia by joining the CIS in 1993, and signing an agreement in 1995 allowing Russia to retain four military bases and up to 20,000 troops in Georgia. These troops are employed mainly in peacekeeping roles in South Ossetia and on the Abkhazian border. In return, Georgia has gained economic aid and Russian mediation in helping to resolve the conflict in South Ossetia.

ECONOMY

UNDER COMMUNISM, Georgians enjoyed a higher standard of living than most people in the Soviet Union, mainly because of the country's pleasant climate and variety of agricultural produce. Today, like many other countries in Eastern Europe and the former Soviet Union, Georgia is undergoing a transition from a rigid, centrally planned economy to an open, free-market economy. These changes have been painful for the republic and have caused many problems: industrial output has decreased, unemployment has increased, and inflation is evident. These factors have resulted in a rapid decline of the standard of living in Georgia.

Above: **Boats at the new sea terminal in Batumi, near the Soviet border with Turkey on the Black Sea.**

Opposite: **French wheat flour being unloaded at the port of Poti.**

The Georgian economy has also been seriously weakened by the conflicts in the autonomous regions of Abkhazia and South Ossetia where many lives have been lost and valuable time and energy wasted. In Abkhazia, economic activity has virtually ceased; half the population has fled the country and many buildings lie in ruins. This is a tragedy for an area that in the Soviet period was one of the wealthiest in the Soviet Union. However, the autonomous region of Adjaria has for the most part avoided conflict and continues to flourish, especially in cross-border trading with Turkey and Armenia.

Because of these problems, Georgia has relied heavily on Russia for economic support, as well as on international bodies such as the International Monetary Fund, which has provided financial aid and advice in an attempt to stabilize the economy. In 1995 Georgia's foreign debt stood at US$1 billion. It became an urgent challenge for Georgia's leaders to revitalize a potentially vibrant and resource-rich economy, especially by attracting foreign investment.

Lining up for bread in Tbilisi. Georgia has been experiencing debt and inflation in recent years.

In 1996 Georgia experienced the beginnings of a promising economic recovery led by the burgeoning private sector. Private industry now accounts for 75% of the republic's gross domestic product and the figure is expected to grow.

FROM PUBLIC TO PRIVATE OWNERSHIP

Under the Soviet system, the Georgian economy was run on socialist principles—public ownership of the means of production (farms, offices, factories, and industry) coupled with a centralized, state-planned economy. In 1994 the government began a campaign of mass privatization, followed in 1996 by legislation allowing for the private ownership of land and regulations for the operation of commercial banks. During the Soviet era, prices of essential goods and services were fixed by the government. Today, the cost of food, gas, electricity, transport, and communications are controlled by market forces and are on a par with world levels.

AGRICULTURE

Forty percent of the land in Georgia is used for agriculture. Under the Soviet system, the traditional, small family farms and estates of the Georgian nobility were replaced by government-run collective farms requiring many workers. Recently most of these farms have been privatized and divided into units for private ownership.

Garden plots have traditionally been popular in Georgia. Under the Soviet system they were viewed by their owners as valuable sources of extra income. During the Soviet period, according to some estimates, as much as 40% of Georgia's entire agricultural output was provided by produce from private plots. In the current uncertain economic climate, many Georgians are surviving on the crops grown on their small, private plots of land.

The new economic opportunities and the emerging private sector have also led to a widening gap between a small, rich elite and the majority whose material conditions have steadily worsened.

TRADING

Georgia trades mainly with other former Soviet republics. Its main exports of grapes and other fruit, vegetables, wheat, barley, wine, brandy, vodka, livestock, light industry, machinery and metalworking equipment, chemicals, metallurgical products, and building materials go mainly to:

Russia	50%	Azerbaijan	6%
Turkey	15%	Ukraine	5%
Turkmenistan	7%	Others	17%

Its main imports of oil, natural gas, machinery, and equipment come from:

Turkmenistan	40%	Ukraine	5%
Turkey	31%	Azerbaijan	2%
Russia	7%	Others	15%

In the countryside, families farm their land without the benefit of modern methods.

The country's exceptionally sunny climate promotes the growing of subtropical crops. Tea and citrus fruits are grown in Adjaria, Guria, Samegrelo, Imereti, and Abkhazia. Wine grapes, tobacco, olives, figs, almonds, apples, pears, and some grains and sugar beets are also grown throughout western Georgia.

The Alazani valley in Kakheti is recognized as the country's premier wine-growing region. Before 1991 Georgia was the leading producer of table wines in the Soviet Union. Plants such as geraniums, roses, jasmine, and basil thrive and are used by the perfume industry.

In the highland areas and on the Kartalinian Plain, the climate favors crops such as barley, oats, apples, plums, and cherries, as well as sheep grazing. Mountainous areas such as Upper Svaneti are used mainly for sheep and goat farming. Nearly a third of the working population is employed in the agricultural industry, making it the largest employer in the country.

OIL—THE GREAT GEO-ECONOMIC GAME

Georgia has little oil itself, but has transport and storage facilities that are used to move oil from neighboring Azerbaijan. Azerbaijan extracts oil from the Caspian Sea, one of the richest sources of oil in the world today. Many American and British oil companies have invested in the oil fields of the Caspian Basin. Georgia recently signed an agreement to expand a pipeline that links Azerbaijan with the Black Sea port of Batumi, which has one oil refinery. From Batumi, the oil is transported by sea to Western markets.

Plans are afoot to extend the pipeline farther east to carry oil from Turkmenistan and Kazakhstan, both oil-producing countries. The link may eventually be extended westward to Turkey, providing quick access to the Mediterranean and then to Europe and the world. Such an arrangement would provide Georgia with a ready supply of petroleum, as well as a vital and profitable interest in the region's most important economic asset.

However, Georgia's plans to provide a link between Europe and the oil-producing countries of Central Asia conflict directly with Russian interests. The Russians have their own pipelines running from Azerbaijan and Kazakhstan through southern Russia to the Black Sea port of Novorossisk. As a major force in the region, the Russians expect to have a say in the major economic assets of former Soviet republics. They also resent Western interference. A compromise was reached in 1995; as a result two pipelines will carry oil westward—one through southern Russia and the other through Georgia.

MINERAL WEALTH

Georgia is rich in resources. There are about 300 known mineral ores in the republic, of which only half are currently being exploited. There are substantial reserves of clay that can be used to make cement and other building products. Since antiquity, Georgia has been famous for its metallurgy. The area around Kutaisi is rich in manganese deposits, a mineral used to make high-grade steel. Copper and lead are present in substantial quantities.

Georgia's main industrial center is Rustavi, a new town 20 miles (32 km) southeast of Tbilisi. Rustavi is a typical industrial town with iron and steel mills and various chemical plants. Here, laminated sheet iron and seamless pipe products are produced.

Throughout Georgia, factories produce diverse products such as farm equipment, locomotives, and tea-gathering machines for the local tea industry.

Since independence, energy has become an expensive commodity. Before 1991, Georgia, as an integral part of the Soviet Union, had all its energy needs met by the other republics. With the breakup of the Soviet Union, however, it now has to buy gas and electricity at the world market rate, and the country has difficulty paying for what used to be heavily subsidized. In the mid-1990s, gas and electricity were rationed, and blackouts became common in urban areas. In rural areas, many people switched to collecting wood to provide heating.

ENERGY

Georgia's mountainous territory has many fast-flowing rivers that provide an abundant source of energy. Over 200 hydroelectric dams have been built to tap the energy of the Rioni, Kura, and Inguri rivers. Nevertheless, most of Georgia's energy is imported. The primary source of energy is natural gas, imported mainly from Turkmenistan. The country also imports most of its oil, although there is an estimated 27 million tons (24 million tonnes) of untapped oil in Georgia. The northwest mountains yield coal, reserves of which are estimated to be about 400 million tons (360 million tonnes). Under Soviet rule, these deposits were not mined because other forms of fuel could be obtained cheaply elsewhere. Exploiting these natural resources to reduce reliance on outside suppliers is one of the most urgent tasks facing Georgia today.

TRANSPORTATION

Georgia has 21,000 miles (33,800 km) of roads and 970 miles (1,560 km) of rail lines.

Three major roads cross the Great Caucasus to provide a link with Russia—the Georgian Military Highway links Tbilisi to Vladikavkaz, another highway links Kutaisi to Vladikavkaz, and a third links Sukhumi to Cherkessk. Armenia, Azerbaijan, and Turkey are linked to Georgia by numerous roads.

President Eduard Shevardnadze believes that the Georgian infrastructure has a crucial role to play in the economic development of the region. The country's roads and ports can provide a bridge for goods and services from the West via Turkey and the Black Sea to the new markets of the Caucasus and Asia. The ports of Batumi, Sukhumi, and Poti were busy import centers in the Soviet period and can regain their influence as the region develops.

Above: **Tbilisi subway station. The country's rugged terrain prevents rail lines from being built across the Caucasus. The main railway line runs along the Black Sea coast linking Sochi in Russia to Sukhumi, then to Kutaisi, and east to Tbilisi and into Azerbaijan.**

Opposite: Dam at the Inguri hydroelectric plant.

TOURISM

Before 1991 the Black Sea coastal resorts were popular vacation spots for people from all parts of the Soviet Union. Every summer Sukhumi, Batumi, Pitsunda, and Gagra would be swamped by people attracted to the warm sea, fine beaches, and sunny climate. The upland areas also offer skiing, climbing, and scenic walks in a fresh mountain climate.

Unfortunately political unrest and recent conflicts, especially in Abkhazia, have destroyed the tourist industry. When the political situation stabilizes, Georgia's beaches and rich cultural attractions have great potential to become a major foreign currency earner by attracting tourists from the West.

GEORGIANS

MODERN GEORGIA IS AN ETHNICALLY DIVERSE country, and many Georgians trace their ancestry to traders, invaders, and refugees from neighboring lands who settled in Georgia over the years. Because the country is mountainous its peoples are broken into many small, independent groups. A 1989 Soviet census listed 96 distinct nationalities in Georgia. Of the 5.5 million people in the country today, Georgians make up 71%. The other major ethnic groups are the Armenians (8.1%), Russians (6.3%), Azerbaijanis (5.7%), Ossetians (3%), Abkhazians (1.8%), and Greeks (1.9%).

During the Soviet period, there was a policy to gradually merge the many nationalities of the Soviet Union into the "Soviet person"—one who would practice socialist principles and put political ideology before national culture. The peoples of Georgia found this ideology unappealing and lost little of their national spirit despite pressure from Moscow.

It is estimated that as many as one million people have left Georgia because of the political and economic hardships of the 1990s. There are large emigré communities of Georgians in Russia, and smaller communities in the United States, France, and Britain.

Left and opposite: **The Georgians dress much like people in other parts of Europe, although fewer designer clothes are sold. During the Soviet period when drab garments were the norm, Georgians still wore their clothes with an elegance that expressed their flamboyance and love of life.**

Georgian woman in an old part of Mtskheta.

KARTVELIAN PEOPLES

The modern republic of Georgia includes three of the four Kartvelian peoples—the Georgians, Mingrelians, and Svans. The fourth group, called Laz, live almost exclusively in modern-day Turkey. The Kartvelian people share a common language, history, and culture. The origin of the Kartvelians as a people is not known, but they are probably the result of a fusion of aboriginal Caucasian peoples with immigrants from Asia Minor.

Nowadays when people refer to Georgians, they usually mean all Kartvelian peoples, including the Svans and Mingrelians. Since 1930 the Mingrelians and Svans have been ethnically classified as "Georgians." This makes the 3.9 million Georgians the most dominant group in the country.

GEORGIANS The Georgians call themselves *Kartvelebi* ("kart-VE-le-bi") and their country, *Sakartvelo*. These names are linked to the mythical demigod, Kartlos (said to be a great-great-grandson of Moses), who is considered the "father" of all Georgians. In the Western world, the country's name is mistakenly believed to have come from its patron saint, Saint George. In fact, "Georgia" originates from "Gurj," the name given to the people of Georgia by the Arabs and Persians.

Physically, Georgians resemble the peoples of the eastern Mediterranean, but they are generally taller with athletic, wiry bodies and dark hair and eyes. They are an elegant and attractive people. The women, especially, have a reputation for being graceful and beautiful. When the Ottoman Turks ruled the country, Georgian women were often carried off to the harems of the sultans.

The Georgians are also proud, passionate, and fiercely individualistic, retaining a strong sense of family. They are renowned fighters with strict codes of personal honor and a long tradition of chivalry. They are welcoming toward guests and travelers and are considered among the most hospitable people in the world. Friendship is highly prized and celebrated in the country's 12th century national epic, *The Knight in the Panther's Skin*, written by Shota Rustaveli.

The people behave and carry themselves with dignity and what many observers consider a sense of royalty. In an unofficial census many years ago as many as one in seven Georgians claimed to be of royal descent.

MINGRELIANS It is estimated that there are nearly one million Mingrelians in Georgia, the majority of whom live in the region of Samegrelo, their traditional homeland in the Kolkhida lowlands. Some people consider the Mingrelians the most beautiful people of the Caucasus because of their fair skin, blond hair, and blue eyes—rarities in this part of the world. Tea production has made the Mingrelians one of the wealthiest peoples in Georgia.

On the hills above Tbilisi is a monumental statue of *Kartlis Deda* ("KART-lis DE-da"), or "Mother Georgia." In her left hand she holds a bowl of wine and in her right, a sword. This statue symbolizes the Georgian character—welcoming toward friends but fierce toward enemies.

SVANS There are approximately 80,000 Svans in Georgia who live mainly in the mountainous regions of Upper and Lower Svaneti. Throughout the Middle Ages, the Mongol invasions, and the Turkish and Persian incursions of the 16th and 17th centuries, the Svans found themselves cut off from the mainstream of Georgian cultural and social life, safe and isolated in their mountain fortresses. Consequently their dialect has much in common with older rather than modern forms of Georgian.

The character of the Svans is very much a product of their harsh, mountainous environment. They are a proud, independent, and hardy people used to a stoical existence with few of the comforts of modern civilization. Hunters and climbers are the most respected members of the community. Vendettas and blood feuds between communities and families continue to this day. However, the Svans, like all Georgians, are very hospitable toward guests and travelers.

ADJARIANS

The people of the Adjarian Autonomous Republic are mainly ethnic Georgians, although the majority are Muslims. This is a result of Ottoman Turkish rule from the 16th to 19th centuries. Many Adjarians still have close cultural and family ties with the bordering Turkish provinces.

ABKHAZIANS

There are approximately 92,000 Abkhazians in Georgia. Despite their small numbers, they are a visible minority because they inhabit their own republic, the Abkhazian Autonomous Republic, along the northwest coast of the Black Sea.

The origin of the Abkhazian people is shrouded in mystery, although they have been in Georgia for about 2,000 years. They are thought to be a proto-Georgian people who, in the 17th century, mixed with the Adige, a northern Caucasian tribe, and in doing so lost their Georgian-oriented culture.

The Abkhazians are ethnically a northern Caucasian people different from the Kartvelian, or southern Caucasian people. They are a mountain people and have traditionally lived as shepherds.

The people have their own government and language, Abkhaz. Russian is spoken as a second language. Few Abkhazians speak good Georgian, although many of those who live in the south of Abkhazia, near Samegrelo, speak Mingrelian, the dialect of that region. Most Abkhazians are Muslims.

Because of the movement of people from other parts of Georgia and Russia in the late 19th and early 20th centuries, the Abkhazians are a minority in their homeland, making up only 18% of the population of Abkhazia. It is because of this imbalance and perceived decline that the Abkhazians have campaigned and fought for independence from Georgia throughout the 1990s.

Above: **Abkhazians being evacuated from Abkhazia, a region of civil unrest.**

Opposite: **Agricultural lifestyle in the region of Upper and Lower Svaneti, where the people have preserved many ancient customs and beliefs.**

Religion and ethnicity have created considerable problems in Georgia. In 1944 Stalin had 144,000 Muslim Georgians from the southwest province of Meskheti transported forcibly to Uzbekistan in Central Asia, a fate suffered by many ethnic groups throughout the Soviet Union in the 1930s and 1940s. Although successive Soviet regimes have acknowledged that these people did not commit any crimes, the now 300,000 Meskhetians in Uzbekistan have not been allowed to return to their homeland. Today Meskheti is populated by Christian Georgians and Armenians from other parts of the country. The Georgian government has so far opposed the return of the exiled Meskhetian Muslims, fearful that an increase in the Muslim population will create further ethnic and religious tension in an already fragile region.

A Georgian Jew belonging to one of the minority ethnic groups in the country.

OSSETIANS

There are about 165,000 Ossetians, of whom only 65,000 live in the South Ossetian Autonomous Region. The Ossetians make up 66% of the people in South Ossetia; 100,000 Ossetians live in other parts of Georgia, in addition to those living in North Ossetia, just across the border in the Russian Federation.

The Ossetians are an Iranian people and are thought to be descendants of the ancient Alans, who came to the region in the 6th century A.D. They are essentially a mountain people and are Muslims, differences that single them out from the Georgians. Many Ossetians would like to withdraw from the Georgian republic and unite their region with North Ossetia. The Georgians, however, believe that South Ossetia is historically a part of Inner Kartli and resist any attempt at separation.

OTHER PEOPLES

Because of the constant movement of people and shifts of power throughout the history of the Caucasus, many other peoples from the surrounding region have settled in Georgia. There are 445,000 Armenians in the country, making them the largest foreign nationality. The Armenians are Christians and have their own language and alphabet. They are spread throughout the world mainly because of historical persecution from the dominant Turkish and Arab Muslims in south and west Armenia. Tbilisi has a large Armenian population, as do the regions of Meskheti and Dzhavakheti.

There are approximately 310,000 Azerbaijanis in Georgia, the majority of whom live south of Tbilisi, in and around the towns of Bolnisi and Marneuli. Most speak Azerbaijani and are Muslims.

About 346,000 Russians have also settled in Georgia, including 75,000 in Abkhazia and 38,000 in Adjaria. There are about 100,000 Greeks in Georgia, living mainly in the western part of the country, and smaller numbers of Ukrainians, Jews, and Kurds.

Theater performers in long plaits wearing the traditional costume for women.

DRESS

Occasionally on festival days, during celebrations, or for the fun of it, the Georgians dress in their distinctive traditional costume. Men wear the *cherkeska* ("CHER-kes-kah"), a knee-length tunic worn with soft, high, leather boots and a *burkah* ("BUR-kah"), or woolen cape, flung over their shoulders. Georgian men like to appear masculine and often wear daggers for special occasions, as well as cartridge cases sewn on the chest of their tunics. In Svaneti and Kakheti cylindrical-shaped woolen caps are traditional. The women also wear *cherkeskas*, although theirs are usually longer than the men's and decorated with etched silver chains and buckles. Many women in the rural areas wear headscarves but this traditional headgear is losing its popularity in the cities.

LIFESTYLE

GEORGIANS ARE TRADITIONAL in their ways, and family and marriage form the cornerstone of society. This traditional lifestyle is reinforced by a strong sense of national identity. Unfortunately the economic realities of the 1990s have seriously affected people's standard of living. Unemployment has risen sharply and food prices have reached astronomical levels. In 1993—one of the worst years politically and economically—80% of the people were estimated to be living below the official poverty line, although things have improved since.

COUNTRY AND CITY LIFE

Life in the cities prospered during the Soviet era, but mountain communities were generally left out of the technological advances made in the lowland areas. This led to a steady drift of people to the cities.

Left and opposite: **Today, 56% of Georgians live in the urban areas and the rest in the country.**

61

Group outing in a park. In Tbilisi, as in many other Georgian cities, most summer activities are held outdoors.

In the cities, it is popular to take a walk after work. People are in the habit of strolling up and down the main thoroughfares in the evening, talking, laughing, and occasionally going into a café for a glass of wine, brandy, or coffee. This custom offers young Georgians the opportunity to meet each other. In Tbilisi the most popular place for taking an evening walk is the tree-lined Rustaveli Avenue. Around this street are Tbilisi's best cafés, restaurants, shops, cinemas, and theaters. Elsewhere, there is always something going on—people buying and selling things, playing games or musical instruments, eating together, or just chatting.

In the villages most people work on the land. It is common for Georgians to have their own fruit or vegetable plots and, in some cases, even vineyards in their back garden. Their lives are dominated by the changing seasons. For example, Kakheti is a hive of activity in October when grapes are harvested. The villagers celebrate the bounty by decorating the balconies of their houses with bunches of grapes, and every available basket and bucket is filled to the brim with grapes.

HIGH LIVING

Georgians regard the mountainous provinces of the Caucasus to be the heart and soul of their country. Many of their traditions are believed to have originated there—the lavish hospitality, codes of honor, and the importance placed on friendship.

The mountainous areas are thinly populated compared with the lowlands. The winter population of places such as Khevi and Mtiuleti is only about 7,000 people in each region. The lifestyle is pastoral and lack the advantages of modern technology. People generally make their living as shepherds and by growing a few vegetables on the limited amount of fertile land. The weather is harsh in the winter months and there are frequent landslides and road accidents. Along many mountain roads it is common to find small, cage-like structures that are memorials marking the spot where someone was killed. Inside each memorial is a picture of the deceased, a bottle of wine, and some drinking glasses. This allows passing friends and relatives to stop and drink to the memory of their loved one.

Enjoying a relaxed life-style.

HOSPITALITY

Hospitality, generosity, and friendship are the codes by which Georgians live. They are known for their uninhibited hospitality, accosting friends and even strangers regularly and inviting them into their homes for an impromptu drink, snack, or meal. Georgian hospitality often means that meals last for hours and consist of many courses, toasts, and lengthy arguments and discussions. Although Georgians love their wine, they consider it bad taste to get drunk. The measure of a man's masculinity is often equated with his ability to hold his drink.

YOUR HEALTH!

The Georgians love to celebrate and take much pride in their toasting. Toasts are always initiated by the *tamada* ("TA-ma-da"), or toastmaster. Once the *tamada* has proposed the toast and drunk, the other guests may follow. If a toast honors a particular person, the assembled guests drink to that person first, allowing the individual to respond with a final toast of thanks. Often a special or honored guest will be presented with a *khantsi* ("KAN-tsi"), a large goat's horn filled to the brim with wine, and asked to drain it all at once. Important toasts usually mean that the glass is drained in a single gulp as a sign of respect. The last toast will be in honor of the *tamada*, and to a safe journey home. As the Georgians would say, *gauma ... jos!* ("ga-u-MA-jos") or cheers!

FAMILY AND MARRIAGE

Traditionally it is the man's family who seeks a bride and initiates marriage negotiations. This is normally done through a female relative who assesses the suitability of unmarried women in the locality. A "chance" meeting will then be arranged to give the pair the opportunity to see each other. If there is some attraction, they will meet again, after which the man or a member of his family approaches the girl's parents to ask for her hand in marriage. When the marriage proposal is accepted, the groom produces a gold ring to mark the engagement. A dowry is given by the bride's family, although this is usually small.

Wedding in a Kakheti village.

Church wedding ceremonies were rare during the Soviet era, but the tradition is gradually being revived with the demise of communism and an increase in religious practice. The main wedding ceremony is a social rather than a religious event. First, the groom goes to the bride's house in a ribbon-decked car, followed by a noisy, colorful convoy of his family members. Following this, the couple go to a registry office to register the

marriage and exchange rings. A celebration at the groom's home follows, which includes dinner, toasts, singing, and dancing, and is attended by the couple's families.

A *tamada*, usually one of the groom's uncles, acts as master of ceremonies. That night, the couple spend their first night together in their own bedroom in the groom's family house. Feasting usually continues for several days. The day after the wedding, the bride is traditionally taken to fetch water from the local spring, where she will have the opportunity to meet the womenfolk of her new neighborhood.

In the past, rural Georgians in particular married someone from their home area, often from the same village. As a result of the increased social mobility that came with being a part of the Soviet Union, marriages among people from different parts of Georgia and even across the Soviet Union became more common.

CENTENARIANS

Georgians, like other Caucasian people, are famous for their longevity. It is a medical phenomenon that has attracted wide interest and for which experts can offer no concrete explanation. The statistics tell the story—the republic claims 51 centenarians for every 100,000 inhabitants.

The centenarians do not merely live a long time, but usually live full lives, working, relaxing, and enjoying themselves as young people do. Longevity is particularly prevalent in Abkhazia, which has a famous choir—*Nartaa* ("NAR-ta")—made up wholly of men aged 70 to 130 years old. *Nartaa* is an amazing sight and performs throughout Georgia, entertaining locals and visitors alike.

Surprisingly, the average life expectancy for men in Georgia is 69 years and for women, 76 years—unremarkable figures compared to the rest of the world. So why are there so many centenarians? Although there is no sure explanation, some observers think it is the Georgians' healthy diet (vast amounts of yogurt, fresh vegetables, and dairy products), healthy mountain air, fresh spring water, beneficial effects of the superior local brandy, and the Georgian love of life.

MALE DOMINATION

Georgia is a male-oriented society where the birth of a baby boy is celebrated over that of a girl. Boys are usually spoiled by their mothers, which contributes to their sense of superiority. Georgian male role models are traditional and often old-fashioned. The most admired men in Georgia are bandits, warriors, and horsemen from the country's eventful past, all of whom are remembered in popular songs and dances. Boys are often named after these popular figures. Such role models influence the men's attitudes and reinforce the image of the macho male. This image is further reflected in the traditional costumes worn by men on special occasions—they are usually decked out in *cherkeska* and carry a sword, dagger, or gun cartridges.

Male and female roles are very clearly defined, and sexual equality is not an issue in Georgia as it is in Western countries. Although not an inhibited race, the Georgians do observe a strict code of sexual morality. The men treat women with great respect, but not necessarily as equals. For example, the men are unlikely to help in household chores such as washing or cooking, which they consider feminine tasks.

Georgian women are traditionally feminine in their behavior and are not likely to be engaged in masculine work or pastimes. The ideal life choice for women is to be a wife and mother. In the cities, more women are financially independent, but are likely to live with their families until they marry, as is the case with their male counterparts.

Above: **Men in national dress. Family ties, camaraderie and friendship are of the highest importance to Georgian men.**

Opposite: **Georgian longevity is attributed to a healthy diet, positive outlook, and love of life.**

Financial problems have meant that independent Georgia can only guarantee free education for the first nine years of school, starting at the age of six. College education has to be self-financed.

EDUCATION

Education has always been important to Georgians, and centers of learning can be traced back as far as the time of the Colchians. For much of history the Georgian church ran the schools, providing the country with an educated class.

Under the Soviet system all Georgians were guaranteed free preschool, primary, secondary, and higher education. As a result, Georgia has one of the highest proportions of college graduates among former Soviet countries. There are 19 colleges in Georgia. Some specialize in teacher training and others in agricultural studies. Also included are a medical school, an art academy, a music conservatory, and a theater-institute—all in Tbilisi. The University of Tbilisi is Georgia's largest institution of higher learning and was founded in 1917 following the Russian Revolution.

WORK AND WELFARE

Georgians work normal office hours, although the shops are open from 8 a.m. to 9 p.m. on most days. The right to strike is recognized by the Georgian constitution. Allowances are given to the unemployed, single mothers, and refugees. However, the amount is so small—just a few dollars a month—that it does not provide an adequate welfare safety net.

All Georgians are entitled to basic health care. Georgia has a high-quality, state-run health system that includes 500 hospitals and more than 17,000 doctors. Unfortunately the government has had problems in recent years finding the money needed to operate the system effectively. Some hospitals are being privatized, offering people a choice of services.

BENDING THE RULES

In the past Georgians always found that the communist system limited their natural exuberance and entrepreneurial spirit. They have a special term—*blat* ("BLAT")—for getting around rules and regulations. The word can be roughly translated to mean obtaining benefits or favors through personal influence instead of by merit or through official channels. In its mildest form it means simple patronage, and in its more extreme form it means outright extortion or fraud. Because of this, Georgians have earned themselves a reputation for black-market trading, especially in Russia.

During the Soviet era, small cottage industries flourished in Georgia, and despite current economic difficulties, these businesses remain fundamental to the Georgian economy and lifestyle. The spirit of *blat* has, unfortunately, manifested itself in a more ominous form since independence, with the rapid growth of criminal, Mafia-type organizations throughout Georgia. The Russians, with some justification, blame the Georgians for some of the criminal activities that have become a feature of post-communist life in Russia.

Although welfare allowances are small and the government has limited resources, it is trying to direct attention to those most in need, especially the elderly.

RELIGION

GEORGIA IS A RELIGIOUSLY DIVERSE country where freedom of religious expression is guaranteed in the 1991 constitution. In Tbilisi, for example, there is a Jewish synagogue, a Muslim mosque, a Georgian basilica, an Armenian church, and a Zoroastrian temple within a 15-minute walk of each other.

Although there is no official state religion, the Georgian Orthodox Church is accorded special importance and is nominally supported by 65% of the population. It is native only to Georgia and has a special place in the national consciousness as an institution that is peculiarly Georgian. Throughout history, and especially in the tsarist and Soviet eras, the church provided a powerful focus for Georgian patriotism and nationalism.

The other main religions in the republic are Islam (11%), the Russian Orthodox Church (10%), and the Armenian Apostolic Church (8%).

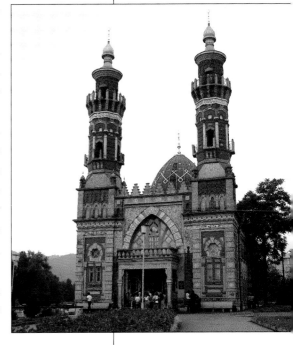

Above: A mosque in South Ossetia.

Opposite: **Part of the rich ornamentation on the Ananuri church fortress built beside the Georgian Military Highway.**

GEORGIAN ORTHODOX CHURCH

Christianity came to Georgia in A.D. 330. The story of the country's conversion is a mixture of fact and legend. Tradition tells that a slave woman, who later came to be known as Saint Nino, cured the Iberian Queen Nana of a strange illness. This proved the woman's holiness and helped her gain the queen's confidence. Legend has it that the queen's husband, King Mirian, was converted when he found himself enveloped suddenly in pitch darkness while on a hunting trip. He then invoked the Christian God, upon which the light of day returned. It is thought that he actually saw an eclipse of the sun and mistook it for a divine event.

In western Georgia Christianity replaced early beliefs based on a pantheon of Greek gods; in eastern Georgia, it replaced an Iranian Zoroastrian religion. The conversion to Christianity had a profound effect on Georgian culture and history. The country suddenly became one of the few Eastern outposts of Christianity with its cultural and social orientation toward Christian Europe, away from the Islamic civilizations to the south and east.

In the 5th century the church became autonomous and appointed its own leader, the Catholicos of Mtskheta. Throughout the Middle Ages the Georgian Church held enormous political and economic power and inspired a tradition of art, architecture, and literature.

Under tsarist rule, however, the church lost its independence and was treated as a branch of its much larger brother, the Russian Orthodox Church. The independent status of the Georgian Church was reestablished during the Soviet era when Stalin—who had trained for the priesthood in Georgia—intervened on its behalf. Despite this, many of the 2,000 churches in Georgia were closed and left to deteriorate, and it is only over the last 10 years that the churches have been reopened and restoration work begun.

PRACTICES The Georgian Orthodox Church is part of the Eastern branch of Christianity, the Orthodox Church, practiced in much of Eastern Europe and Greece. The Eastern churches split formally from Western Christianity in the 11th century and do not recognize the Pope in Rome as their head, nor observe any of the Western church's holy days. The Orthodox churches have never had a central body or leader, as the Catholic church does. The current head of the Georgian Church is Catholicos Illya II. Georgian Orthodox practice is similar to that of the other Orthodox

Late 19th century Russian religious icon found in Georgia.

churches, although it differs in some of its liturgical rules and rituals. Christmas and Easter are the most important days in the Georgian Orthodox calendar.

Superficially, Orthodox practice has more in common with Catholic than Protestant practice. Ritual is important and includes music, the burning of incense, and chanting. Icons are positioned around the inside of most churches, and walls are covered with frescoes depicting religious events. Believers pray in front of the icons, lighting candles as offerings and often kissing the icons as a mark of devotion. Orthodox services are usually sung in Georgian. The combined experience is intended to convey the essence of Christianity, appealing to worshipers' emotional, intellectual, and esthetic faculties.

Since the late 1980s, there has been a revival of faith in Georgia, especially among the rural population. More children are being baptized, and church weddings are becoming popular. The government has encouraged the revival as a healthy expression of the national spirit. The president, Eduard Shevardnadze, was recently baptized, taking on the new Christian name of "Georgi."

Georgia's patron saint, Saint George, pictured slaying a dragon. November 23 is celebrated as Saint George's Day.

SAINT GEORGE

Saint George is the patron saint of Georgia and icons showing him slaying a dragon are widely found in Georgian churches. In pagan times the worship of heroes and warriors was common. Saint George, as a strong and dashing warrior-saint, was the ideal figure to fill this role after the country's conversion to Christianity, and he is revered even today.

CHURCH OF THE LIFE-GIVING PILLAR

The Cathedral of Sveti-tskhoveli in Mtskheta is one of the most sacred places in Georgia. The site was chosen for one of Georgia's first churches in the 4th century because it was the burial place of an early Georgian saint, Sidonia. A cedar tree grew from the grave, and King Mirian ordered seven columns to be made from its trunk to provide the church's foundations. It is said that upon completion of the sixth column, the seventh rose magically by itself into the air and could only be put into place when Saint Nino interceded through prayer; also that a sacred liquid flowing from the column could cure all diseases. In Georgian *Sveti* ("SVE-ti") means "column" and *tskhoveli* ("ts-KOV-el-i") means "life-giving."

RUSSIAN ORTHODOX CHURCH

Christianity reached Georgia before it reached Russia; the Georgian Orthodox Church is older than the much larger Russian Orthodox Church by about six centuries.

In Georgia 10% of the people are Russian Orthodox Christians. Russian Orthodoxy originated from Kievan Rus (the kingdom of Rus originally centered around Kiev) in the 10th century when Christianity first came to Russia. Over the next few centuries it became the religion of all Russians. In the 19th century it was brought to Georgia by Russian and Ukrainian migrants from tsarist Russia. The tsarist authorities encouraged the establishment of monasteries in an attempt to strengthen their influence in the region as part of their Russification policy. One of the most famous of these is Novy Afon (New Athos), built in Abkhazia in 1900. Russian churches are found mainly along the coast of the Black Sea, and in the larger cities such as Tbilisi and Kutaisi.

The Russian Orthodox Church is the largest Eastern church and is the chief representative of the precepts of Orthodoxy. The head of the church is the Patriarch of All Russia.

The unusual shape of the Georgian cross is ascribed to Saint Nino. It is said that upon entering Georgia, she took two vine branches and tied them into a cross using strands from her own hair, thus producing an imperfectly shaped cross.

THE VARDZIA CAVES

The Vardzia Caves, spectacularly situated 10,000 feet (3,000 m) above sea level in the Lesser Caucasus, form a vast complex of man-made cave dwellings, palaces, churches, and monasteries. The caves are carved out of soft tufa and were begun as secular dwellings in the 5th century B.C. They were expanded by a Christian religious community in the 8th and 9th centuries A.D., and Queen Tamar used the caves to create a monastery and a center of Georgian culture in the late 12th century.

The Vardzia Caves represent the apex of cave architecture and a supreme expression of the Georgian religious spirit. Some of the 500 or so individual cave dwellings have their own small churches. The centerpiece of the complex is the Church of the Assumption, carved out of the cliff in 1184 on the instructions of Queen Tamar. The church contains many magnificent frescoes as well as inscriptions and portraits dedicated to the queen and her father, King Giorgi III. The most monumental religious fresco is that of the Virgin and Child. Other frescoes on religious themes include portrayals of the crucifixion, descent into hell, and raising of Lazarus.

A fresco in a church. The Armenian church differs in dogma and practice from both Georgian Orthodoxy and mainstream Orthodoxy.

ARMENIAN APOSTOLIC CHURCH

The Armenian Apostolic Church is marginally older than the Georgian Orthodox Church and was founded in the late 3rd century by Gregory the Illuminator. In converting the Armenian king, Gregory in effect created the world's first truly Christian state. The Armenian Church separated from the other Eastern churches in the 6th century and is autonomous. It is headed by the Catholicos of Echmiadzin near Yerevan, Armenia.

Armenian churches tend to have simple decorations. They practice the custom of suspending ostrich eggs from the ceilings of the churches as symbols of hope and resurrection. Georgia contains the largest community of practicing Apostolic Armenians outside Armenia. Armenians first began migrating to Georgia in the 14th and 15th centuries as a result of persecution by the Muslim Turks and Arabs.

ISLAM

Islam is a major religion in the Caucasus—many of the peoples in the Russian regions north of Georgia are Muslim, as are the populations of Turkey and Azerbaijan. Georgia has historically been perched on the northern edge of the Islamic world, and the religion has left its mark on the republic. Georgia's Azerbaijani population are Muslims, as are the Abkhazians, Ossetians, and most of the ethnic Georgians in Adjaria.

JUDAISM

Anti-Semitism is virtually unknown in Georgia, and there have been Jewish communities in the country since the Middle Ages. The largest Jewish communities are in Kutaisi and Tbilisi; smaller groups can be found in the mountain regions. At one time 2% of the population of Kutaisi was Jewish, although over the last 10 years the Jewish presence has been reduced significantly by massive emigration to Israel.

Muslims at prayer. The Islamization of Georgia's coastal areas occurred under the rule of the Ottoman Turks, who occupied parts of Adjaria until the mid-19th century.

LANGUAGE

WITHIN THE SMALL AREA of the Caucasus there are an enormous variety of languages. Consequently many languages are spoken in Georgia. The Roman writer Pliny recorded in the 1st century A.D. that the Romans needed 130 different interpreters to do business in the Caucasus. Strabo, the ancient Greek geographer, records in the same period that as many as 70 different languages were spoken daily in the market in Dioscuris (modern-day Sukhumi).

Georgian is the most widely spoken of the Caucasian languages. It is the official language of the Georgian republic and is spoken as a first language by approximately 70% of the population. Other local languages are spoken domestically in the various regions.

GEORGIAN

Georgian belongs to the Kartvelian (South Caucasian) family of languages, which also includes Mingrelian, Laz, and the archaic Svan. All these languages originated from Old Kartvelian (circa 2,000 B.C.). Georgian does not fit into any of the major European language groups; despite numerous attempts, no one has managed to establish a genetic relationship between Georgian and any other language or language family, even within the Caucasus. The Caucasian languages are grouped together for geographical convenience rather than linguistic similarity.

Of the more than 70 Caucasian peoples—excluding the Armenians— only the Georgians had a written language of their own before Russian

Above and opposite: **The durability of the Georgian language has probably contributed more than any other factor to the survival of Georgian culture and the Georgians as a people.**

colonization in the 19th century. Because of Georgia's turbulent history, Greco-Roman, Persian, Arabic, Turkish, and most recently, Russian, have all left their mark on the language.

Russian was the only compulsory language taught in Georgian schools in the Soviet era. Following independence, however, learning Georgian has become compulsory for all Georgians, and all main curriculum subjects are taught in Georgian.

REGIONAL DIALECTS The Georgian literary standard is based on the language of the Kartli region around the capital, Tbilisi. However, Georgian includes a number of regional dialects: Imeruli (spoken in Imereti), Rachuli (spoken in Racha), Guruli (spoken in Guria), Khakuri (spoken in Kakheti), and Acharuli (spoken in Adjaria). Minor dialects are also spoken in some of the remote mountain regions such as Pyavi, Khevsureti, Tusheti, and Mtiuleti.

Georgian is the most common language of communication in many parts of Georgia. Learning Georgian is compulsory in the schools, but for political reasons, such a policy is difficult to enforce in the troubled regions of Abkhazia and South Ossetia.

HISTORY OF THE GEORGIAN LANGUAGE

The Georgian alphabet was originally developed to aid the spread of Christianity. Christianity became the official religion of Iberia (modern-day Kartli and Kakheti) and Armenia in the 4th century A.D. The Iberians used Greek and Syriac texts for worship, but soon found a pressing need for a vernacular language to spread the new religion. A commission was set up to produce an alphabet that would represent the sounds of the Georgian and Armenian languages. In the 5th century a system of writing based on the Greek alphabet was developed. The oldest Georgian inscriptions discovered date from 430 A.D. and were found in a church near Bethlehem in Israel.

Georgian texts have traditionally been grouped under three periods: old Georgian (5th to 11th centuries), medieval Georgian (12th to 18th centuries), and modern Georgian (18th century to the present). Medieval Georgian reached its zenith in the periods of David the Builder and Queen Tamar, especially in the work of Georgia's greatest lyrical poet, Shota Rustaveli.

Georgia only began to recover from the ravages of the Mongol conquest in the 18th century, and a unified literary language developed and flourished in the 19th century under Russian guidance. Ilya Chavchavadze (1837–1907), the famous writer, did the most to modernize and promote the developing Georgian literary language. In the same period Jacob Gogebashvili (1840–1912) wrote *The Georgian Alphabet* (1865) and the definitive book on the Georgian language, *Native Speech* (1876).

Shota Rustaveli, a 12–13th century portrait from a manuscript in the State Art Museum of Georgia.

81

Georgian text outside a cinema.

Under the Soviet system, Georgian was recognized as a state language of one of the Soviet Union's constituent republics and was consequently allowed to flourish with institutional support.

THE GEORGIAN ALPHABET

Since its adaption into a written form, Georgian has progressed through three alphabet systems. The one used today is called *Mxedruli* ("m-ked-RU-li"), meaning "secular writing," so called because in the 11th century it replaced a script called "church writing." The spelling for *Mxedruli* script is straightforward; each letter has its own pronunciation and each sound always corresponds to the same letter. There are no long vowel sounds in Georgian.

There are 33 letters in the modern Georgian alphabet, including five vowels and 28 consonants. There is no distinction between upper and lower case letters. As with most languages, Georgian is written from left to right.

PRONUNCIATION GUIDE

Mxedruli script	*Mxedruli* script transliteration	Simplified English pronunciation
ა	*a*	similar to the short *a* in *hat*
ბ	*b*	pronounced as the English *b*
გ	*g*	pronounced as the English *g*
დ	*d*	pronounced as the English *d*
ე	*e*	similar to the short *e* in *pet*
ვ	*v*	pronounced as the English *v*
ზ	*z*	pronounced as the English *z*
თ	*t*	pronounced as the English *t*
ი	*i*	similar to the short *i* in *hit*
კ	*k'*	pronounced as the English *k*, but glottalized
ლ	*l*	pronounced as the English *l*
მ	*m*	pronounced as the English *m*
ნ	*n*	pronounced as the English *n*
ო	*o*	similar to the short *o* in *hot*
პ	*p'*	pronounced as the English *p*, but glottalized
ჟ	*zh*	pronounced as the letters *si* in *vision*
რ	*r*	similar to a rolled *r*
ს	*s*	similar to a soft *s*, as in *hiss*
ტ	*t'*	pronounced as the English *t*, but glottalized
უ	*u*	similar to *oo*, as in *hook*
ფ	*p*	similar to the *p* in *pot*
ქ	*k*	similar to the *k* in *kit*
ღ	*gh*	similar to the *ch* in *loch*, but pronounced with a vibration
ყ	*q'*	similar to the English *k*
შ	sh	similar to the *sh* in *shirt*
ჩ	ch	similar to the *ch* in *church*
ც	ts	similar to the *ts* in *pits*
ძ	dz	similar to the *dz* in *adze*
წ	*c'*	similar to the *ts* in *pits*, but glottalized
ჭ	ch	pronounced as the *ch* in *church*, but glottalized
ხ	kh	similar to the *ch* in *loch*
ჯ	*j*	similar to the *dge* in *edge*
ჰ	*h*	pronounced as the English *h*

In the early medieval period Georgian speakers from eastern Georgia crossed into Adjaria and Guria and drove a wedge between the Laz and Mingrelians, who consequently lost touch with each other and developed along separate linguistic lines.

LEARNING GEORGIAN

Georgian is a complex language that is difficult to learn. It contains a complex set of rules governing verbs, as well as many formidable clusters of consonants—for example, Tbilisi—("t-BLI-si")—that can baffle and frustrate the foreign student. Other examples are *trtvili* ("TR-t-vi-li," meaning "frost") and *brtskinvale* ("br-ts-kin-VA-le," meaning "brilliant"). Georgian also includes many glottal stops, similar to the sound English Cockneys make when they say "bottle" ("BOH-aw"). Vowels are short and sharp, and the people roll their r's.

Fortunately all 33 Georgian letters correspond to only one sound each so confusion should not arise. Where there are two or three syllables in a word, the stress usually falls on the first syllable. For words with four or more syllables, the situation is more complicated.

OTHER TONGUES

There are many ethnic groups in Georgia and just as many languages that are spoken as either a first or second language.

MINGRELIAN, LAZ, AND SVAN These belong to the Kartvelian group of languages and are closely related to Georgian. Mingrelian is spoken along the central and southern coastal areas of the Black Sea, mainly in Samegrelo. Laz is spoken mainly in parts of Georgia close to northeastern Turkey. Mingrelian and Laz were originally subdivisions of the ancient Colchian tongue.

Svan has no alphabet and is spoken mainly at home and socially by the small mountain communities of Svaneti. Svan has preserved more of old Kartvelian than Georgian, probably because of the isolation of the Svans at various times throughout history.

In the 1930s the Mingrelian and Svan people were classified collectively as Georgians and their languages categorized as Georgian dialects. Since then, the Mingrelians and Svans have received their education in Georgian and are classified as Georgian speakers.

ABKHAZIAN There are about 90,000 speakers of Abkhazian in the Abkhazian Autonomous Republic. The 1991 constitution recognizes it as the state language of Abkhazia. Abkhazian is a member of the small northwest Caucasian family of languages that includes Circassian and the almost extinct Ubykh, still spoken in parts of Turkey.

Abkhazian is not related to the Georgian language and many Abkhazians speak poor Georgian, preferring instead to use Russian as a second language. The first Abkhazian alphabet was devised in 1862, but a wide selection of publications in Abkhazian became common only during the Soviet period. Television programs have been broadcast in Abkhazian since 1978.

Georgian is a pleasant language to listen to and can sound impressive when spoken eloquently.

DIVIDED BY MANY TONGUES

Language	Spoken as a first language	Spoken as a second language
Georgian (including Mingrelian)	3,900,000	270,000
Russian	340,000	1,700,000
Ossetian	130,000	—
Armenian	370,000	—
Azerbaijani	300,000	—
Abkhazian	92,000	—
Svan	80,000	—

OSSETIAN, AZERBAIJANI, AND ARMENIAN Ossetian, the language of ethnic Ossetians, is spoken in various parts of Georgia, especially in South Ossetia. It is part of the Iranian group of languages. Azerbaijani and Armenian, the national languages of Georgia's two neighbors, are spoken by Azerbaijanis and Armenians living in Georgia.

RUSSIAN As the language of the Soviet Union and of the tsarist authorities that preceded the 1917 revolution, Russian has been spoken in Georgia for 200 years. Today it is still a popular *lingua franca* for those communities—such as the Ossetians, Abkhazians, Armenians, and Azerbaijanis—who do not speak Georgian well.

NAMES

As can be expected in a country with many ethnic groups, Georgians are named according to their ethnic and linguistic background. Georgia's Muslim population—such as the Azerbaijanis, Ossetians, and Abkhazians—often take traditional Islamic names, while the Russians and Armenians use names from their own languages.

Popular Georgian men's names include Georgi, Nerab, Shota, David, Pavele, Alec, and Soso. Popular female names include Marina, Tamara, Lamara, Tamriko, Tsitsi, Thea, Lili, and the ubiquitous Mary.

Many Georgian surnames end in *idze* or *adze* (meaning "son of"), or *vili* (meaning "child").

PUBLICATIONS, RADIO, AND TELEVISION

For a country with a long literary tradition, it is not surprising that Georgia has many newspapers and periodicals. Since the *glasnost* period of the late 1980s and subsequent independence, there have been a steady number of new periodicals and newspapers.

There are about 150 newspapers published in Georgia, of which 120 are in Georgian. The principal newspapers in Georgian are *Young Iberian, Literary Georgia, Native Land, Free Georgia, Georgian Herald*, and *Republic of Georgia*. There are also newspapers published in Russian, Armenian, Abkhazian, and Ossetian. Of the 75 periodicals in Georgia, 60 are in Georgian.

Georgia's national radio and television networks are government-owned and controlled. Radio shows are broadcast in Georgian, Russian, Armenian, Azerbaijani, and English, while television programs are in Georgian and Russian.

This Georgian baby may grow up speaking many languages, for there is no lack of media communication to cater to the needs of the various communities in Georgia.

ARTS

GEORGIA HAS A RICH ARTISTIC HERITAGE stretching as far back as the second millennium B.C. It has been able to absorb the artistic influences of neighboring Turkey, the Middle East, and Russia, while retaining a style and an expression that is strictly Georgian. In Georgia, art has rarely been used as a vehicle for social change but has provided the fiercely independent Georgians with a means of expressing their national character and affirming their cultural independence.

METALWORK

The Georgians were fabled in the ancient world for their skill at metallurgy. Finds in tombs at Trialeti show that the Bronze Age Georgians were highly accomplished at smelting, forging, soldering, and embossing articles to a high level of precision. In the 4th and 5th centuries, Georgian jewelry was second to none in the ancient world.

Following Georgia's conversion to Christianity, iconography and book illumination—which saw handwritten books being illustrated or decorated as an art form—became popular from the 8th century A.D., and represent some of the world's earliest examples of the medieval goldsmiths' skill. The 10th century Ishkani Processional Cross and Khobi Icon of the Virgin Mary, and the 11th century Martvili Cross and silver roundel of Saint Mamai from Gelati, are some of the beautiful pieces that can be seen in the Georgian State Museum in Tbilisi. The most famous piece in the museum is the 10th century Khakhuli Triptych embossed with rubies, pearls, and enamel. The triptych is a masterpiece of medieval craftsmanship and was believed to have miraculous powers.

Above: **Woven carpets and rugs, some of the local craft of Georgia.**

Opposite: **Building in Mtskheta decorated with Georgian folk art motifs.**

ARCHITECTURE

Georgians appear to have an affinity with stone and their architecture combines the practical and the picturesque. There are many cathedrals, churches, monasteries, castles, and fortifications throughout Georgia.

The most popular style of dwelling is the rustic house known as *darbazi* ("dar-BA-zi"), dating back to ancient times. The center of the *darbazi* tapers into a pyramid made from wooden logs, with successive layers piling up to form a chimney at the top. Modern variations of these can be found in central Georgia, usually decorated with beautifully carved doors, lintels, and fireplaces.

CHURCH ARCHITECTURE Georgian religious architecture thrived in the golden age of King David the Builder and Queen Tamar. Two designs for churches were popular: the domed type and the basilica. Domed churches have either a square or hexagonal-shaped central section. Basilica churches have a large rectangular center with aisles on each side.

Variations of the domed church first appeared in Georgia in the 6th and 7th centuries. The most famous of these is the Church of Dzhvari, situated spectacularly on a cliff at the confluence of the Aragvi and Kura rivers a few miles from Tbilisi. The famous Cathedral of Sveti-tskhoveli (Church of the Life-Giving Pillar) can be found at Mtskheta. It is a basilica-type church built in the 11th century. The arcaded interior walls are covered with grotesque beasts carved in stone. The story of the building of this church is told in Constantine Gamsakhurdia's historical novel, *The Hand of the Great Master.*

The Alaverdi Cathedral in Kakheti and Bagrat Cathedral at Kutaisi also date from the 11th century. The well-known Gelati Monastery was founded by King David the Builder in 1106. The monastery complex consists of three churches, an academy building, and the tomb of the king, who had also intended the monastery to be a center of learning. The development of religious architecture came to an end with the Mongol invasion in the 13th century.

Vardzia cave town in the mountains.

FORTRESSES AND CAVE TOWNS Because of the many conflicts fought on Georgian soil, it is impossible to go very far in the republic without coming across a fortress or castle. Situated on the Solalaki Ridge and dominating the skyline above the old section of Tbilisi are the ruins of the massive Narikala Fortress. The towers and walls were built by Arab lords in the 8th century on the site of fortifications erected by King Vakhtang Gorgasali. The strategic importance of this fortress was such that King David the Builder—and after him the Mongols, Turks, and Persians—all rebuilt and extended the fortifications, making it a hybrid of styles. Part of the fortress was destroyed when gunpowder stored there was struck by lightning in 1827.

Ananuri is a superb 16th century fortress complex situated near the Georgian Military Highway 40 miles (64 km) north of Tbilisi. Its crenellated walls and defensive towers make it one of the more memorable monuments along the highway. The fortress was built by the dukes of Aragvi, a violent feudal family, as a residence and sanctuary during their frequent feuds with rival dukes.

Georgia has some very impressive cave architecture, rivalled only by similar dwellings in the Middle East. Uplis-Tsikhe, south of Gori in Kartli, is a city made of caves carved into the soft stone of the cliffs and hills overlooking the Kura River. It grew over a period of hundreds of years in the first millennium B.C. The city continued to flourish throughout antiquity and was an important trading center in the Middle Ages with a population of 20,000. It was sacked by the Mongols in the 13th century and never regained its former importance. The weather has slowly eroded the cave city, although the shapes of the dwellings and the city walls are still visible.

The caves were used as a place of worship; an impressive church basilica dates from the 9th century. Uplis-Tsikhe served as a prototype for the cave monasteries that developed later at David-Garedzha and Vardzia. David-Garedzha is a complex of 12 monasteries built amid the semilunar landscape of the Garedzha Hills in Kakheti, a few miles from the Azerbaijan border.

Upper Svaneti's stone watchtowers served as homes as well as a military fort.

WATCHTOWERS OF UPPER SVANETI

In the remote mountain region of Upper Svaneti, many traditional peasant houses have an unusual feature: a 90-foot (27-m) stone tower. The earliest towers date from the 12th century. Although built as a defensive structure that allowed the Svans to see their enemies approaching from a distance, the size of a tower also indicated the power and standing of a family within the community. Each tower traditionally has four floors—the first for storing fodder and livestock, the second for religious devotions, and the third and fourth for the family and garrison. The towers are remarkably sturdy and have withstood landslides and avalanches that have swept away much newer buildings. It is thought that this is because egg yolk was used in the mortar.

93

King Vakhtang VI supported literature in the early part of the 18th century.

RUSSIAN INFLUENCES   Because of the tsarist Russification policy, Russia's neo-Classical style imposed itself in the 19th century. However, the Russians' strict notions of classical order were subverted by the flamboyant charm of the Caucasus and a hybrid style developed. Many of these hybrid buildings can still be seen in Tbilisi.

Many large, ugly municipal buildings sprang up under the Soviet regime. The only contemporary construction of any note is the building of the Ministry of Highways in Tbilisi, built in 1977. Paradoxically, Oriental styles from Georgia and other Central Asian Soviet republics influenced building styles in Soviet Russia as well. Examples include the "wedding cake" type of architecture seen in Moscow's Hotel Moskva.

LITERATURE

Georgia has an independent literary tradition that dates back to the 5th century A.D. when a distinctive Georgian alphabet came into being. The earliest works of Georgian literature were historical and religious, translating biblical and scriptural texts and describing the lives of Georgian saints. Jacob of Tsurtaveli's *The Martyrdom of St. Shushanik* (476–483) is the earliest of these. The earliest Georgian chronicle, the *Conversion of Iberia* written in the 7th century, describes the mission of Saint Nino. Georgian writing of this period was also influenced by contact with early Christian and Arabic literature, and many Persian tales were recast in Georgian form.

In Shota Rustaveli's epic masterpiece, *The Knight in the Panther's Skin*, Georgian medieval literature reached its zenith. Written during Queen Tamar's illustrious reign, this long epic poem embodies the cultural sophistication of the period and reflects the influence of Chinese, Persian, and ancient Greek philosophy. It has a universal appeal and has been translated into most major languages.

After the Mongol invasions of the 13th and 14th centuries, Georgian cultural and artistic life stagnated. Georgian literature eventually revived in the 16th century, renewing its ties with Muslim oriental verse. In the early part of the 18th century, King Vakhtang VI (1675–1737), a poet and scholar, codified Georgia's laws in the *Code of Vakhtang*, and set up Georgia's first printing press.

Following Russian annexation, Prince Alexander Chavchavadze (1787–1846) and Gregor Obeliani (1800–83) were the first representatives of a thriving Romantic movement among the Georgian aristocracy. In the 19th century, many Georgian intellectuals studied in Russia and traveled throughout Europe, gaining greater exposure to new ideas. Despite heavy tsarist censorship, Georgian writers turned to social themes in the latter part of the 19th century, reflecting many of the political concerns current in Russia and Europe at the time. Two leading figures in this movement

ABKHAZIAN WRITING

Abkhazian literature came into being at the end of the 19th century. An Abkhazian alphabet was first created in 1862 and the first Abkhazian newspaper was printed in 1919. Dmitri Gulia (1874–1960) was a major promoter of Abkhazian writing and culture and founded Abkhazian prose with his short story, *Under Alien Skies,* in 1919. Samson Chanba (1886–1937) wrote in both Abkhazian and Russian, and his plays draw on themes from revolutionary history. Fazil Iskander (b. 1929, pictured at right), a contemporary writer from Sukhumi, writes in Russian and is distinguished for his subtlety, humor, and philosophical character. His poetry collections and novella, *Kozlotur's Constellation*, have been widely read in Russian-speaking countries.

were the writers Ilya Chavchavadze (1837–1907) and Akaki Tsereteli (1840–1915). In the early 20th century, the Georgian symbolist poets experimented with new forms of poetic expression. Among this group were Paolo Iashvili (1895–1937), Titsian Tabidze (1895–1937), and Galaktion Tabidze (1891–1959), whose movement, *The Blue Horns*, thrived in the years of the Georgian independence struggle, 1918–21. However, Georgian national literature was suppressed during Stalin's reign and Titsian Tabidze was executed during one of the purges of the 1930s, while Iashvili committed suicide.

Georgian literature slowly revived following the death of Stalin. Constantine Gamsakhurdia (1891–1975) was the greatest novelist of the immediate post-Stalinist period and introduced an unprecedented subtlety to Georgian prose. He explored Georgia's past and culture through historical novels such as *The Hand of the Great Builder* (1942–62) and *The Flowering of the Vine* (1955).

Otia Ioseliani (b. 1930) is a successful contemporary dramatist whose comedies *Until the Ox Cart Turns Over* and *Six Old Maids and a Man* have been staged in Germany. Chabua Amirejibi (b. 1921) is noted for his narrative power on historical themes, while Otar Chiladze (b. 1933) explores Georgian myth and history through his novels. Lia Sturua (b. 1939) is Georgia's best-known contemporary woman poet.

Ilya Chavchavadze did much to modernize and promote the Georgian literary scene in the late 19th century.

PAINTING

Painting is a relatively recent art in Georgia, flourishing since the end of the 19th century. Niko Pirosmanishvili (1862–1918), popularly known as Pirosmani, was a self-taught artist who painted in a direct, primitive style. Through his depiction of everyday Georgian life at the turn of the century, he expressed the national psyche better than any other Georgian artist. He died in obscurity and his work was recognized only after his death. His paintings, such as *Woman and Children Going to Draw Water*, can be seen in the Georgian State Art Museum in Tbilisi.

Georgian painting flourished under the Soviet regime. Mose Toidze (b. 1902) painted in the Socialist Realist style promoted by the Soviet authorities. Lado Gudiashvili (1896–1980) and David Kakabadze (1889–1952) both painted in a distinctly Georgian style. Gudiashvili is famous for his fantastic and grotesque portrayals, especially *Fish* (1920) and *The Underprivileged* (1930). Kakabadze created skillful abstract works. Helena Ahklevediani (1901–76) is known for her depictions of historic Tbilisi.

The Feast of the Three Nobles by Georgian artist Niko Pirosmanishvili.

97

MUSIC AND BALLET

Tbilisi has long had musical connections. Zakaria Paliashvili (1872–1933) is considered the father of Georgian opera. His most famous works are *Abesalom and Eteri* and *Daisi*. Tbilisi's marvelous Moorish opera house, the Paliashvili Opera and Ballet Theater, was named in his honor. His contemporary, Meliton Balanchivadze (1862–1937), is also considered one of the originators of Georgian professional music. He wrote the country's first national opera, *Perfidious Daredzhan*, first staged in Tbilisi in 1926. His son, Andrei Balanchivadze (b. 1906), continued the family's musical tradition by writing the first Georgian ballet, *Heart of the Hills,* in 1936, and *The Pages of Life* (1961).

Dmitri Arakishvili (1873–1953) brought Georgian folk music into the mainstream, writing and composing more than 500 pieces. He also composed a number of symphonies and choral works.

Vakhtang Chabukiani (b. 1910) is Georgia's most famous ballet dancer and choreographer. After a distinguished dancing career, he became director of the ballet troupe at the Paliashvili Opera and Ballet Theater, where he created a unique style of male stage dancing that combined the movements of both classical ballet and Georgian folk dancing.

FILM

Under the Soviet regime a strong Georgian movie industry developed and prospered. A former sculptor, Mikhail Chiaureli, helped the Georgian branch of Soviet cinema develop in the 1920s and 1930s.

In the post-Stalin era cinema is the only artistic field where Georgian genius has reached its former heights. Like many other forms of artistic expression in Georgia, cinema became a way for people to celebrate their national spirit and culture. Many talented directors have worked in the Gruzia movie studios in Tbilisi. Giorgi Shengelaya (b. 1937) directed *Pirosmani* (1971), a movie that celebrates the life of the famous painter; *Eliso*, based on a short story by Alexander Kazbegi; and *The Blue Mountains*, a satire on Soviet bureaucracy.

Tengis Abuladze, director of the movie, *Repentance*, with actress Ketevan Abuladze.

The most famous movie to come out of Georgia in the *perestroika* (restructuring) period was *Repentance* (1984), an allegory that achieved notoriety for its grotesque depiction of the repressive era under Stalin. Directed by Tengis Abuladze, the movie attracted record audiences all over the Soviet Union, with 17 million people seeing it within the first three weeks of its release. Abuladze had previously won a prize at the Cannes Film Festival in 1956 for the movie, *Magdan's Donkey*, a collaboration with his childhood friend, Revez Chkeidze (b. 1926). He also won the Lenin prize for his trilogy, *The Plea, The Wishing Tree*, and *Repentance*.

LEISURE

ABOVE ALL ELSE, Georgians like to enjoy life. There is a well-known Georgian legend that says much about Georgian attitudes, lifestyle, and leisure. The tale tells of how the Georgians came to possess the country they deem the most beautiful in the world. When the world was being created, God was allotting land to the peoples of the world. The Georgians, who were too busy eating, drinking, and having a good time, turned up late. "There's no land left," God told them. "But we were drinking a toast to your health," answered the Georgians. "Come and join us." It is said that God enjoyed himself so much that he gave the Georgians all the land he had been saving for himself. This tale says much about the Georgians' high regard for their homeland.

When the Georgians are not eating, drinking, and entertaining, they enjoy the kind of leisure activities that are common throughout the world. Radio and television are popular, and people often visit some of Georgia's many museums—especially in Tbilisi—that display the country's rich cultural and artistic heritage. In the summer there are many parks and nature reserves where people can walk, climb, or picnic. The most famous of these are at Pitsunda, Borzhomi, and the Forest Park of the Sukhumi mountains.

Above and opposite: **Georgia's beautiful mountains, lakes, and beaches are enjoyed as much by Georgians as they are by tourists.**

SONG AND DANCE

Many Georgian national characteristics emerge in the people's dancing, which is elegant, lively, and flamboyant. Traditional dance is still a part of everyday life in the republic, and Georgians of all ages need very little excuse to begin dancing—they dance on any and every occasion.

Traditional dance has a
following, even among
the young.

Traditional Georgian dance is chiefly masculine in form, although a few dances are exclusively for women.

The male dances are energetic, involving much high-kicking, leaping, twisting, and acrobatics. The *Fundruki* ("FOON-dru-ki") is a traditional dance performed by men on the tips of their toes. The *Khorumi* ("Ko-ru-mi") is performed by a circle of men. The dance movements portray combat scenes; the men rear up like horses or creep as though hiding behind rocks. The women's dances are less energetic, reflecting a more passive role. The women move their bodies slowly and gracefully. The *Lekouri* ("le-KO-u-ri") is a courtship dance performed by men and women. The dancers do not touch, but circle cautiously, flirting with each other.

Almost every village and valley has its own traditional songs and dances. Often the dances are based on a dramatic local or national occurrence from Georgia's long and eventful history. Folk song and folk dance have developed together in Georgia.

The republic has many professional song and dance ensembles, including the Georgian State Dancing Company, the Rustavi Choir, and *Nartaa.* The Rustavi Choir specializes in restoring the folk music traditions of Georgia, scouring the country for half-forgotten songs that they decipher and record before setting to music.

MOUNTAIN SPORTS AND PASTIMES

Skiing is a popular pastime in Georgia. Situated in Kartli in the Lesser Caucasus, Bakuriani is one of the chief ski resorts and was, in the Soviet era, one of the most popular and famous downhill skiing complexes in the Soviet Union. The resort is 6,000 feet (1,800 m) above sea level and has been compared to Squaw Valley in the United States for its ideal climate and conditions. Another major ski resort is at Gudauri, north of Tbilisi on the Georgian Military Highway. Built and operated as a joint Georgian-Austrian venture, Gudauri is a sparkling new complex of hotels, sports facilities, and superb downhill runs.

Climbing is also a popular sport and attracts both locals and international climbers. Because of its high peaks, Upper Svaneti is a popular place to climb and has produced some of the most famous mountaineers in Georgia. One of the best-known was Mikheil Khergiani (1932–69), who died in a climbing accident. His house in Mestia has been turned into a museum in honor of his achievements. His father, Beknu Khergiani, has the distinction of being the climber who removed the Nazi flag from the top of Mount Elbrus after it had been planted there by the advancing Germans in 1943.

Nartaa members in a friendly arm-wrestling bout.

103

Another popular spot for alpinists and explorers are the slopes of Mt. Kazbek, especially because of the great number of legends and myths associated with the mountain. One legend says that the Georgian Prometheus, Amirani, was chained in a cave on the mountainside as punishment for giving fire to mankind.

OTHER SPORTS

As in many parts of the world, soccer is Georgia's most popular sport, with home games played in the capital's 75,000-capacity National Stadium. In the 1970s and 1980s, the Dinamo Tbilisi team won championships in the

CHESS

Throughout the former Soviet Union, chess is a very popular pastime, and Georgia is no exception. The Georgians have been very successful in international competitions and the women, in particular, have excelled in international chess. Nona Gaprindashvili was the women's world champion for 16 years, from 1962 to 1978. She was eventually ousted from her long reign by another

Georgian, Maya Chiburdanidze, who became the women's world champion at the age of 17. Chiburdanidze reigned as women's world champion for 13 years, from 1978 to 1991. Gaprindashvili and Chiburdanidze have the distinction of being the only two women to hold the title of Grandmaster in both women's and men's chess.

Among the men, Tamaz Georgadze has performed well in international and Russian competitions, and won the international title of Grandmaster in 1977. Since the breakup of the Soviet Union, Georgia has fielded its own chess teams at international competitions and is ranked among the top 10 countries in the world for the sport.

Soviet league and played in European competitions. Kutaisi, Batumi, and Sukhumi also have well-supported soccer teams. Georgia produces many top-class soccer players, many of whom have moved abroad to play in the major European leagues in Germany and England. Georgia has its own rugby federation and rugby is becoming increasingly popular.

Georgia boasts its own unique form of wrestling. Part sport and part dance, the wrestling is unusual because it is performed to music. It resembles judo in that the contestants are not permitted to use choke-holds or fight while lying down. Georgians have also gained wrestling honors on the world stage. As a part of the Soviet team, Levan Tediashvili was both Olympic and World champion in the 1970s.

A number of traditional folk games are still played. *Tskhenburti* ("ts-KEN-bur-ti," or "horse ball") is played on horseback by both men and women. It is similar to polo, which is also popular.

In addition to Georgia's own Black Sea health resorts, Sochi in neighboring Russia, also on the Black Sea coast, is a popular summer destination.

HEALTH RESORTS

Georgia's Black Sea coast is the location of many resort towns and beaches, and this is where many Georgians like to spend time relaxing, especially in the summer. During the Soviet era, government departments from all over Russia had holiday homes reserved for the use of their staff, and every summer people from all parts of the Soviet Union descended upon Georgia's beaches.

Known as Bichvinta in Georgian and Pitsunda in Russian, the republic's most famous Black Sea resort was named after the unique pine grove indigenous to the area. The pine grove borders a 4-mile (6.4-km) stretch of beach that is packed each summer. The sunny Abkhazian climate, the beach, the pleasant smell of pine needles, and a 10th century church make Pitsunda one of the most sought-after resort towns. Because of the conflict in Abkhazia, it is less accessible than it used to be, although the cessation of hostilities should ensure its continued popularity.

BATH TIME

Tbilisi is famous for its hot sulfur baths. Rich in hydrogen sulfide, the waters have curative effects appreciated by locals and travelers over the centuries. The baths have been associated with Tbilisi throughout its history and are said to be the reason King Vakhtang Gorgasali moved his capital here. In the 12th century as many as 68 different baths drew upon the plentiful underground waters.

There are many sulfur baths in Tbilisi, but the best-known is the Herekle bath, situated underground and covered with a grand, domed roof. Many Georgians go to the baths to relax and subject themselves to a rigorous body massage. This includes being laid on a stone slab, having their bodies slapped and pummeled, being rubbed with a horsehair mitten (to remove dead skin cells), soaped, and finally rinsed with a bucket of warm water.

French author Alexandre Dumas (1802–70), in *Adventures in Caucasia*, describes the experience: "Suddenly, when I least expected it, two attendants seized me, laid me out on a wooden bench and began to crack every single joint in my body, one after the other. Although I felt no discomfort, I was convinced they were all dislocated, and half expected that at any moment, these silent Persians would fold me up like a towel and pop me away in a cupboard. Then one of them held me still while the other positively danced up and down my whole body. He must have weighed a hundred and twenty pounds or more, but he seemed as light as a butterfly. A great sense of freedom and well-being permeated me. All my tiredness had gone and I felt strong enough to lift a mountain."

BORZHOMI MOUNTAIN RETREAT Borzhomi is immediately identified with the curative spring water of the same name, well-known inside and outside of Georgia. Situated in the beautiful Borzhomi Gorge in southwest Kartli on the River Kura, the town of Borzhomi is the largest and best-known mountain spa in the country. The town is home to numerous sanatoriums to which many Georgians go in the summer for a three-week "cure." The fresh mountain air, curative mineral waters, pleasant climate, and rich forests provide the ideal atmosphere for rest and recreation. Georgians swear by the healing effects of the water, which is also a popular drink.

The town was originally created by the Russians in the 19th century, and they quickly discovered it to be the ideal retreat from the stresses of running an empire. Russian influence is reflected in the 19th century carved wooden houses.

"Never in my life have I encountered either in Russia or in Turkey anything more luxurious than the Tiflis baths."

—Alexander Pushkin, (1799–1837), Russian poet, on the Tbilisi baths. Tiflis is the old name for Tbilisi, transliterated from Russian.

FESTIVALS

DURING THE SOVIET ERA many festivals—such as Labor Day, Soviet National Day, and World War II Victory Day—were celebrated in common with the rest of the Soviet Union. Since independence, however, traditional Georgian festivals have been revived. The old, Soviet-inspired festivals are now celebrated on a much smaller scale or have been dispensed with altogether. The patriotic Georgians prefer to celebrate their own folk festivals and those linked to the Georgian Orthodox Church.

Although the Soviet Union was officially atheist and religious festivals were frowned on, the popularity of the Georgian Orthodox Church never truly declined. The Georgian Church became, to some extent, a focus for Georgian nationalism during the Soviet era. It is no surprise, then, that with the demise of the Soviet Union and Georgia's ensuing independence, Orthodox festivals have sharply increased in popularity and are celebrated with great enthusiasm.

Above: **Soloist from the Imedi folk dance group.**

Left: **Musician at the Kolhoba festival celebration at a village in Adjaria.**

Opposite: **Georgians can be seen sporting their national dress during festivals.**

109

Woman decorating an Easter egg.

GEORGIAN ORTHODOX AND FOLK HOLIDAYS

Some folk and religious holidays are celebrated nationally, while others are peculiar to a town or region. In keeping with the spirit of a people who enjoy feasting, almost all religious services and festivals are followed by a meal and festivities in the town or neighborhood square, and drinking and toasting continue late into the night.

The Georgian Orthodox Church celebrates all the major feast days of the Orthodox calendar. The Georgian Church, like the Russian Orthodox Church, follows the Julian calendar, which is 13 days behind the Gregorian calendar used by most of the world.

The Feast of Saint Basil the Great is celebrated on January 1 throughout Georgia. Saint Basil (329–379) was one of the great spiritual fathers of the Eastern Orthodox Church and because of this is feted throughout the Orthodox world. Along with other Orthodox countries, Christmas is celebrated on January 6, according to the church calendar.

Easter is by far the most important festival in the Georgian Orthodox calendar, as it is for all Orthodox churches. Women and children prepare and dye Easter eggs, a symbol of renewal and rebirth. As with all Georgian festivals, family and friends gather after the church service to celebrate with a feast. Ascension Day—commemorating the ascension of Christ into heaven—is observed 40 days after Easter. Candles are extinguished as part of the church ritual to symbolize Christ's physical departure from this world.

Saint Nino, who introduced Christianity to Georgia, is honored in May. Church services and feasts also mark the Birth of Saint John the Baptist on June 24, and the Remembrance of Saints Peter and Paul on June 28. The Assumption—Saint Miriam's Day—is celebrated on August 28 in memory of the death of the Virgin Mary and the belief that she was bodily taken up into heaven.

Mtskheta's Day is observed on October 14. Mtskheta is Georgia's oldest city and the center of ancient Iberian culture. The Georgians believe that the city was named after Mtskhetos, son of Kartlos, the mythical father of the Georgian people. On Mtskheta's Day, the congregation throngs the Cathedral of Sveti-tskhoveli. This is one of the most sacred places in Georgia and the center of the Georgian Orthodox Church. The patriarch leads a procession around the cathedral grounds, carrying banners and icons. Bells are rung to celebrate the occasion. In the town, the people are entertained by clowns, mime artists, and wrestlers.

Saint George, the patron saint of Georgia, is honored on November 23. This is a very popular feast day because he is not only a Christian symbol but also a national figure who represents the country's warlike pre-Christian past.

Painting of Christ at Georgia's Lavia Monastery.

Many folk festivals are celebrated locally at various times of the year. On the third Sunday after Easter, for example, a special holiday in honor of Saint George is celebrated in Tbilisi and many parts of Kartli, Kakheti, Imereti, and Svaneti. Another festival is *Okanoba* ("o-ka-NO-ba"), held to mark the day Iberia adopted the Christian faith. This occurs in Gori and other parts of Kartli on the second day of Easter.

In the major wine-producing regions of Kakheti and Imereti, it is traditional to hold festivals and celebrate the harvest when gathering the grapes in October. Balconies and windows are decorated with bunches of grapes, and songs and dancing take place when the day's work is done.

OTHER RELIGIOUS FESTIVALS

Georgia's Muslim population celebrates all the major Islamic festivals, such as *Id-ul-Fitr*—a celebration to mark the end of the fasting month of Ramadan—and *Id-ul-Adha*, Prophet Mohammed's birthday. Georgia's small Jewish community celebrates all the major Jewish festivals.

CIVIL HOLIDAYS

Georgians still celebrate a number of civil holidays that have survived from the Soviet era. May 1 is celebrated as Labor Day throughout the Commonwealth of Independent States and in Georgia, is a popular spring holiday.

Georgians also observe World War II Victory Day on May 9 by laying wreaths and paying their respects to those who lost their lives in the war. During Soviet rule it was the practice to have holidays to celebrate the achievements of certain public services, such as industry or the military. Some of these days are still observed, such as Georgian Police Day (November 22), which includes a parade of police vehicles through Tbilisi.

TBILISOBA

The Festival of Tbilisi, *Tbilisoba* ("t-BLI-so-ba"), occurs on the last Sunday in October. It was specially created by the Soviet authorities to celebrate Tbilisi and all things Georgian, as an official expression of the national spirit. The festival is marked with a street carnival, and many of Georgia's famous song and dance ensembles put on traditional Georgian performances. The celebration is not complete without the traditional personification of old Tbilisi—the roguish Kinto—clowning with a wine skin.

Unfortunately the festival has been suspended in recent years following the tragic killing of 20 demonstrators in Tbilisi by Soviet special forces on April 9, 1989. The suspension is a sign of protest and national mourning. There is talk of the festival being reinstated in future.

Mothers' Day has replaced the more politicized Soviet celebration of International Women's Day in March.

Street parade during a Tbilisoba festival.

INDEPENDENCE DAY Georgians celebrate their independence on May 26. The day marks their country's first independence in 1918 following the 1917 Revolution and the subsequent disintegration of tsarist Russia. Traditionally and historically, this date is more significant to the Georgians than their break with the Soviet Union in 1991.

In recent years Independence Day has been marked by noisy displays of military strength with troops, artillery, and tanks parading down Rustaveli Avenue in Tbilisi, while warplanes fly overhead. In the early 1990s various paramilitary groups, such as the *Mkhedrioni*, participated in the official procession. More recently the *Mkhedrioni's* absence is a positive sign of the waning power of the warlords and the growing strength and stability of Eduard Shevardnadze's democratically elected government.

FOOD

GEORGIAN FOOD MAY BE little-known in the West, but it is one of the most varied and subtle of cuisines in the former Soviet Union. Although Georgian cooking has a distinct flavor, the ingredients and style bear some similarity to the cuisines of the eastern Mediterranean.

The country's sunny climate and fertile soil have traditionally resulted in an abundance of homegrown agricultural produce. Most food is bought fresh from the market. Georgians are not used to eating frozen or processed food. Although multinational fastfood outlets selling hamburgers and fried chicken are known in Georgia, they have yet to achieve the kind of popularity they have in the West, or in other countries in the Commonwealth of Independent States, such as Russia. Classic Georgian ingredients include lamb, chicken, fish, hazelnuts, walnuts, corn, pomegranates, plums, grapes, kidney beans, peppers, coriander, and mint. There are many regional variations.

Above: **A Georgian-style meal.**

Opposite: **Market day in Tbilisi.**

THE GEORGIAN TABLE

Although there are many good restaurants in Georgia's towns and cities, the best place to experience the full range of Georgian cuisine is in the home. Georgians love entertaining and invite relatives, colleagues, friends, and even strangers into their homes at the slightest opportunity. Entertaining at the table offers Georgians the chance to express their generosity, exuberance, and sense of community. For Georgians, a good meal is a well-attended table groaning under the weight of vast amounts of food and drink.

At home women cook and serve the food. The men do not help, but sit instead at the head of the table toasting and entertaining guests. Georgian food is not served in conventional courses or even in any particular order. Soup may make its appearance an hour into the meal, and great platefuls of *shashlyk* ("shash-LIK"), or skewers of grilled lamb, and roast pork may appear late in a meal.

MEAT Georgia is a predominantly mountainous country where people mostly raise sheep and chicken, and this is reflected in the cuisine. *Shashlyk*, better known elsewhere as shish kebab, is the most popular meat dish in the Caucasus, although chicken is also popular. *Chakhobili* ("cha-ko-BI-li") is a chicken and tomato stew spiced with coriander, while *tabaka* ("TA-ba-ka") is cooked by frying chicken that has been pressed between two clay plates. *Khinkali* ("KIN-ka-li"), or dumplings filled with ground lamb, chicken, or beef, is a local favorite. *Basturma* ("BAS-tur-ma") is a thinly sliced and seasoned air-dried beef.

VEGETABLE DISHES Although the Georgian diet is heavily meat-based, vegetables accompany most meals. *Pkhala* ("p-KA-la") is a spiced spinach dish mixed with walnuts and vinegar, and topped with pomegranate seeds. It is generally eaten with *matsoni* ("MA-tso-ni"), or Georgian yogurt and *lavashi* ("LA-va-shi"), a flat, flaky bread.

Lobio ("LO-bi-o") consists of kidney beans baked with water and then crushed with a pestle and mixed with coriander and spices. This is often eaten as an accompaniment to meat dishes. Eggplant is also a popular ingredient. *Badrijani* ("bad-RI-ja-ni") consists of baby eggplants stuffed with ground hazelnuts and herbs, served whole. *Chanakhi* ("CHA-na-ki") is a mixture of eggplants, tomatoes, green peppers, and chunks of lamb cooked in a clay pot. Vine leaves stuffed with rice, herbs, and minced lamb are a popular dish throughout the Caucasus and are served with yogurt.

A serving of popular Adjarian meat and vegetable dishes.

SAUCES Sauces are used extensively at the Georgian table to complement, rather than mask, the primary ingredient. *Satsivi* ("SA-tsi-vi"), better known as the Turkish Circassian sauce, is made of ground walnuts and generally used to accompany poached chicken. *Adzhika* ("AD-zi-ka") is a hot condiment from Abkhazia made from red chilies and herbs, while *tkhemali* ("t-KE-ma-li") is a spicy plum sauce considered an essential accompaniment for *shashlyk*. Pomegranate chutney is also used to accompany lamb and fish dishes.

CHEESE AND BREAD Georgian cheese is generally made from goat's milk. There are many varieties, but *suluguni* ("su-LU-gu-ni") is a typical Georgian cheese that resembles mozzarella. *Khachapuri* ("kach-A-pu-ri") is a cheese pastry made by wrapping *suluguni* cheese in pieces of dough and baking them. This local equivalent of fastfood is sold by street vendors and in cafés and restaurants. Bread is served as an accompaniment to all meals. Called *puri* ("PU-ri"), it is either round and crusty or long and dough-like. The latter variety is known as *dedaspuri* ("de-das-PU-ri"). *Lavashi* (the flat, flaky bread) is often eaten with yogurt.

SHASKLYK

1 onion, chopped
1/4 cup mixed olive oil and vegetable oil
1 bay leaf
1 clove garlic, crushed
2 tablespoons finely chopped parsley
1 teaspoon dried oregano

1/4 teaspoon ground black pepper
Pinch of cayenne pepper
1 cup dry red wine
2 pounds (1 kg) cubed lamb
20 small white onions
2 red peppers, cored and cut into squares

Place onion, oil, bay leaf, garlic, parsley, oregano, black pepper, and cayenne pepper in a thick plastic bag. Pour the wine in, hold the bag tightly to seal the top and shake vigorously to combine. Add the cubed lamb and tie the bag. Refrigerate for 24 hours.

Drain the lamb, but keep the marinade. Thread the lamb on to long skewers, alternating the pieces with small onions and red peppers. Preheat a grill. Place the skewers about 4 inches (10 cm) from the heat. Cook for 10–15 minutes, or until the meat is well browned. Turn regularly, basting with the marinade. Serve with rice and chutney.

DRINKS

Georgia's varied climate means that the humid regions of Samegrelo and Adjaria are able to grow subtropical plants like tea, while the dryer central and eastern parts of the country can grow grapes for winemaking. Georgian tea is of the green variety, and is drunk at home and in tea houses. Thick, strong, Turkish coffee is also popular. Because of Turkey's historical influence in Adjaria, the best place to drink coffee is in one of Batumi's many cafés.

Georgia also produces its own brandy and mineral water. Georgian brandies are considered equal in quality to some of the more famous labels from neighboring Armenia. The best-known labels are Vardzia, Sakartvelo, Tbilisi, and Eniseli. Georgia's own mineral water, Borzhomi—from the resort of the same name—is similar to Perrier, although saltier and less fizzy. Borzhomi has a daily yield of 110,000 gallons (500,000 liters) of mineral water which is sold throughout the world. *Chacha* ("CHA-cha"), a homebrewed spirit made from grape pulp, is drunk in the home.

Above: **Selection of Georgian soft drinks.**

Opposite: **Suluguni**, a cheese made from goat's milk.

119

WINE Georgia has a long winemaking tradition. Archeological evidence suggests that wine was made as far back as 5,000 B.C., making Georgia one of the ancient centers of viticulture. The most famous winegrowing regions are Kakheti, Imereti, Racha, and Lechkhumi. Abkhazia also produces some good wines. Although most of the wine is produced on farms, many residents of these regions have their own garden grapevines, as well as huge tubs for treading the grapes and vats for fermenting the wine. The grapes are harvested in early October.

Georgia grows over 500 grape varieties—a vast array for such a small country—and produces 60 different wines. Protected by the Caucasus, the republic's numerous valleys—each with its own micro-climate—have ideal conditions for growing many types of grapes. The best grape varieties are Saperavi, Tsinandali, Chinuri, Mtsvane, and Tasitska. Most Georgian wines are named after the region or town in which they are produced.

The most popular white wines are Gurdzhaani and Tsinandali; the latter is the pride of Georgian wines and is grown in the Alazani Valley in Kakheti, a region famous for its good wines. The most popular red wines are Mukuzani, Napareuli (both made from the Saperavi grape), Ojaleshi, and Khvanchkara. The last of these has the dubious distinction of being Stalin's favorite. Rkatsiteli is a dry white wine produced in Kardanakhi in Kakheti. Among Georgian wines, it claims the peculiar distinction of being fermented in clay jars buried underground—a unique Kakhetian practice.

During the Soviet era, Georgia produced a large part of the domestic wine consumed in the Soviet Union. However, if Georgian wine producers want to break into world markets, they will have to tailor their wines to a standard that is internationally acceptable.

Opposite: **In Kakheti, jars are being prepared for the new season's wine.**

GEORGIA

RUSSIAN FEDERATION

Pitsunda Cape • Gudauta
Novy • • Sukhumi
Afon **ABKHAZIA**
Bay of Sukhumi
Klukhor Pass
UPPER SVANETI
Mt. Ushba
Mt. Shkhara (16,627 ft / 5,066 m)
Kodori
SAMEGRELO
LOWER SVANETI
Mamison Pass
Mt. Kazbek ▲ • Kazbegi
Krestovy Pass
Black Sea
Inguri • Zugdidi
LECHKHUMI
RACHA
SOUTH OSSETIA
• Gudauri
Central Lowlands
• Kutaisi
Georgian Military Highway
• Tskhinvali
• Ananuri
Rioni
• Poti
GURIA IMERETI
Kartalinian Plain
• Gori
KHEVI
• Mtskheta
Gombori Range
Alazani
• Telavi
• Khashuri
Kura
• Kobuleti
ADJARIA
• Batumi
• Borzhomi
Kura
• Bakuriani
TBILISI
• Rustavi
• Gurdzaani
Iori Plateau
• Vardzia
Lesser Caucasus
• Bolnisi
Iori

TURKEY

ARMENIA

AZERBAIJAN

● Capital city
• Major town
▲ Mountain peak

Feet	Meter
16,500	5,000
9,900	3,000
6,600	2,000
3,300	1,000
1,650	500
660	200
0	0

0   25   50   75 Miles
0   25   50   75   100 Kilometers

QUICK NOTES

OFFICIAL NAME
Republic of Georgia

LAND AREA
26,900 square miles
(69,670 square km)

POPULATION
5.5 million

CAPITAL
Tbilisi

MAJOR CITIES
Kutaisi, Batumi, Sukhumi, Poti, Tskhinvali, and
Khashuri

HIGHEST POINT
Mt. Shkhara (16,627 feet/5,066 m)

MAJOR RIVERS
Rioni, Kura, and Inguri

TRADITIONAL GEOPOLITICAL REGIONS
Abkhazia, Upper Svaneti, Lower Svaneti,
Lechkhumi, Racha, Samegrelo, Guria, Adjaria,
Imereti, Meskheti, Tori, Dzhavakheti, Trialeti,
Inner Kartli, Lower Kartli, Zrtso-tianeti, Khevi,
Mtiuleti, Pyavi, Khevsureti, Tusheti, and Kakheti

CURRENCY
Georgian coupon
(US$1 = 1.25 million coupons; end of 1995)
New currency introduced September 1995: lari
(US$1 = 1.30 lari)

OFFICIAL LANGUAGES
Georgian and Abkhazian
(Russian is also spoken widely)

MAIN EXPORTS
Food (grapes and other fruit, vegetables, wheat,
barley, livestock, wine, brandy, and vodka);
light industrial goods; machinery and metalworking equipment; metallurgical products;
chemicals; and building materials.

MAJOR RELIGIONS
Georgian Orthodox, Islam, Russian Orthodox,
and Armenian Orthodox

IMPORTANT ANNIVERSARY
May 26 (Independence Day)

IMPORTANT LEADERS
King David the Builder (reigned 1089–1125);
    defeated the Turks and restored Georgian
    national unity.
Queen Tamar (reigned 1184–1212); under her
    rule, Georgian religion and arts underwent
    an unprecedented renaissance.
Noe Zhordania (1868–1953); leader of inde-
    pendent Georgia just after World War I.
Joseph Stalin (1879–1953); a native of Georgia
    and remembered as one of history's most
    notorious dictators, he ruled the Soviet
    Union for 31 years.
Eduard Shevardnadze (b. 1928); former Soviet
    foreign minister and Georgia's current
    president.

GLOSSARY

blat ("BLAT")
Bending the rules.

brtskinvale ("br-ts-kin-VA-le")
Brilliant.

Catholicos
Head of the Georgian Orthodox Church.

chacha ("CHA-cha")
Strong, homebrewed spirit made from grape pulp.

chakhobili ("cha-ko-BI-li")
Chicken and tomato stew.

cherkeska ("CHER-kes-kah")
Knee-length tunic.

darbazi ("dar-BA-zi")
Rustic houses dating back to ancient times.

gaumajos ("ga-u-MA-jos")
Cheers!

Kartvelebi ("kart-VE-le-bi")
Georgians' name for themselves.

khantsi ("KAN-tsi")
Large goat's horn filled with wine.

khinkali ("KIN-ka-li")
Bell-shaped dumplings filled with ground lamb, chicken, or beef.

lavashi ("LA-va-shi")
Flat, flaky bread.

Mxedruli ("m-ked-RU-li")
Georgian script.

Nartaa ("NAR-ta")
Famous choir made up of elderly men.

puri ("PU-ri")
Bread.

Sakartvelo ("sa-KART-ve-lo")
Georgians' name for their country, and a term used for the united kingdom of Georgia, first formed in A.D. 1008.

satsivi ("SA-tsi-vi")
Turkish Circassian sauce.

suluguni ("su-LU-gu-ni")
Typical Georgian cheese.

tamada ("TA-ma-da")
Toastmaster.

Tiflis
Old name for the capital, Tbilisi, transliterated from Russian.

Transcaucasia
Collective name for the countries of the Caucasus: Georgia, Armenia, and Azerbaijan. Transcaucasia was a republic within the Soviet Union from 1922 to 1936.

trtvili ("TR-t-vi-li")
Frost.

BIBLIOGRAPHY

Bitov, Andrei. *A Captive in the Caucasus.* London: Collins Harvill, 1992.

Boyette, Michael and Raneli. *Soviet Georgia.* New York: Chelsea House Publishers, 1989.

Clark, Mary Jane Behrends. *The Commonwealth of Independent States.* Connecticut: Millbrook Press, 1992.

Fasel Iskander. *Gospel According to Chegem.* United States: Vintage Books, 1984.

Nasmyth, Peter. *Georgia: A Rebel in the Caucasus.* London: Cassell, 1992.

Roberts, Elizabeth. *Georgia, Armenia, and Azerbaijan.* Connecticut: The Millbrook Press, 1993.

Rosen, Roger. *The Georgian Republic.* Hong Kong: The Guidebook Co. Ltd., 1992.

Russell, Mary. *Please Don't Call it Soviet Georgia.* London: Serpent's Tail, 1991.

Suny, Ronald Grigor. *The Making of the Georgian Nation.* Indiana University Press, 1988.

INDEX

INDEX

INDEX